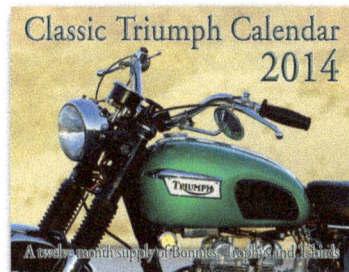

Triumph Motorcycle Restoration - Pre-Unit

Garry Chitwood
Timothy Remus

Published by:
Wolfgang Publications Inc.
Stillwater, MN 55082
www.wolfpub.com

Triumph Motorcycle Restoration - Pre-Unit

Legals

First published in 2009 by Wolfgang Publications Inc., PO Box 223, Stillwater MN 55082

ISBN-13: 978-1-941064-16-0

Printed and bound in U.S.A.

Acknowledgements

The book is nearly done, and it's time for the thank-yous.

First and foremost, I have to thank Garry Chitwood. For assembling two motorcycles, for sharing his wealth of Triumph knowledge with me, and for stopping in the middle of a hundred assembly sequences so I could take just one more photo.

On these pre-unit assemblies we had two helpers. The right-hand-man, the one who can find exactly the right fastener for the frame – before Garry realized he needs it – is Danny Sharder. The other helper, the one without any grey hair, is Danny's son James. James often gave up his day off and after-work evenings to help uncle Garry and that Yankee from up north assemble the TR6 or Bonneville.

They say that behind every successful man there's a hard working woman. In this case the woman who made sure the crew had enough Budweiser is Patricia Chitwood. I'm thankful to Patricia not only for the liquid refreshment, but also for her southern hospitality, and all the help she gave both Garry and I during the writing of the book. For additional help with captions I thank Patricia's side-kick, Susanne.

And without a certain intense bundle of energy named Bobby Sullivan none of this would have happened. Thank you Bobby.

To round out the book a little we added a chapter on Buying a Used Triumph, and another on How to Keep 'em Running. When it comes time to buy a new/old Triumph, there is no one who knows more about what to watch out for than Randy Baxter from Baxter Cycle. Randy is the man who's sold more vintage Triumphs than anyone alive, and he gave freely of his experience in helping me compile a list of dos and don'ts.

If you already own an old Triumph and just want to know more about using it as a regular ride, the man of the hour is Mitch Klempf from Klempf's British Parts. Mitch laid out the rules for anyone who actually wants to ride one of these bikes, instead of just letting them sit in the garage or the living room.

Once again I've assembled a whole pile of images and captions into what I hope is a useful how-to book. Processing all those photos and placing all those captions is the work of Jacki Mitchell, resident graphic artist and computer guru. And to ensure that the captions and copy follow the rules of grammar I thank the lovely and talented Mary Lanz.

Timothy Remus

Introduction

This whole business of publishing Triumph material started some years ago, back in Daytona Beach during Bike Week. In those days a bunch of us stayed in motels and condos down on the south end of the beach, almost to the Port Orange bridge. There was a certain character there named Bobby Sullivan, and despite the fact that I traveled to Daytona to photograph custom Harley-Davidson's, Bobby soon had me photographing vintage bikes that looked nothing like a Harley-Davidson. These bikes did have two cylinders and two wheels, but that's about all they had in common with the more popular brand from Milwaukee.

From that first photo shoot grew the Classic Triumph Calendar, which I'm pleased to say is still in production all these years later. Next came a couple of photo books featuring Triumphs, Triumphs and more Triumphs.

How-to books are way more work than a photo or history book, and it wasn't until 2007 that I took the plunge, with help from the co-conspirators already mentioned nearby, to do a restoration book. That book covered the unit-650cc twins produced from 1963 to 1970.

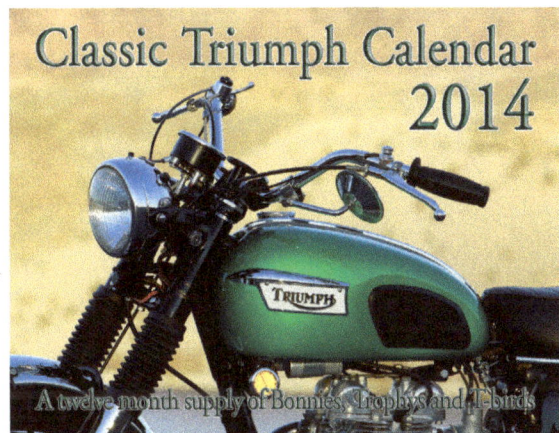

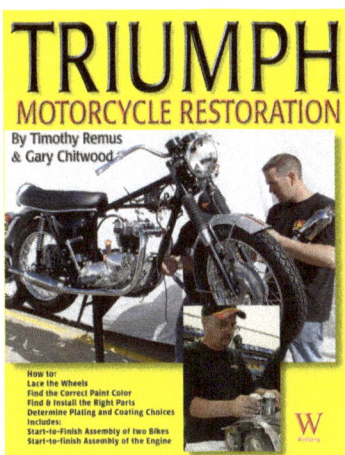

My idea at the time was to create a restoration book that relied on photo sequences instead of just copy, to guide non-professionals in the restoration and repair of old motorcycles. And now we've taken the same concept and applied it to the 650cc bikes produced before 1963, the pre-unit bikes.

The book you hold includes two start-to-finish assemblies, one on a 1956 TR6 and the other on one of the mythical 1959 Bonnevilles. The book also includes one engine and transmission assembly, and the already mentioned chapters on Buying an Old Triumph, and How to Keep 'em Running. As always we've also included a few of side-bars on everything from paint to what it really takes to do a good restoration.

The only thing we didn't include is some of the torque and clearance specifications, meaning you might want to have a factory service manual on the bench, along with this photo guide to Triumph pre-unit restoration, when you tackle that first big Triumph project.

Chapter One

Disassemble the 1956 TR6

Strip it to the Bare Bones

Before starting on the disassembly of the two-wheeled wonder you just brought home from the auction, there are two things you need; a table or hoist that gets the bike up off the floor, and a digital camera.

Take plenty of photos. Whether the bike you brought home is pretty nice, or pretty trashy, the photos will prove a valuable resource when it comes time to put this whole thing back together again. It's also a good way to answer questions about hardware that might have been missing when you started on the project.

The TR6 we started with looks pretty complete here, which makes the restoration that much easier because we have most of the parts, and we know they actually fit the bike. Which is not always the case when you build a bike from used and aftermarket parts.

The other thing you need is some boxes. Cardboard boxes and a marker. The boxes will help you keep the parts in logical groupings, the sheet metal parts in one and the hand controls in another, you get the idea.

The boxes are also a good way to organize the work that will need to be done before the reassembly. In other words, put the parts that need paint in one group, and anything that will need to go to the cad plater, or the chrome shop, in another. Speaking of cad plating, the local chrome shop may not perform this service, but likely will know someone who does.

The actual disassembly is pretty straight forward. As shown here, take off the sheet metal first, followed by the controls. Take time to inspect the parts you take off, check the condition of the gas tank for example. Is the bottom of the tank solid, how much work will the tank need before it's ready for paint?

Remember that on these older bikes the primary drive needs to be disassembled first. Then the engine and transmission can be unbolted from the mounting plates and pulled from the frame.

Once the bike is reduced to a pile of parts, take a good inventory. Based on that inventory you can finalize your decisions as to which parts need to be replaced, which go to the various outside shops, and which you can clean, repair and possibly paint yourself.

Garry sends all his frames and chassis components out for powder coating. He likes the durability of the powder paint, an especially nice feature if you have any thoughts of riding the bike at a later date.

The outside shops you use for paint and plating are often busier than you think. Painters in particular are notorious for dancing to their own drummer. So don't let the sheet metal sit in the garage until two weeks before you want to assemble the bike, get if off to your painter of choice sooner, rather than later.

A really good restoration requires really good attention to detail, and the ability to stay focused and organized. This way everything gets done according to the schedule and nothing is lost along the way.

We take the tank off first…

…followed by the the exhaust, oil tank and tool box. The headlight and handlebar controls are next…

…and then the fenders.

After the front fender is off, along with a few small components, we do an inventory of the parts...

You have to pull apart the primary drive, so the engine and transmission can be taken out separately.

...and a list of any that might be missing. In particular, I watch for missing or incorrect fasteners.

We're finally down to a bare frame.

Be sure to group all the parts separately. Small components and fasteners can be kept in clear plastic bags.

Once it's all laid out, double check your inventory. Decide what's missing, which parts need paint and which need polish or plating. Extra time taken now will pay dividends when it comes to the assembly.

Q&A Garry Chitwood

Can a regular person restore a Triumph at home?

Yes, they need a set of basic tools, and some specialty tools too. They can buy the special tools from someone like Mitch Klempf, Randy Baxter or John Healy (see Sources). Things like Wentworth wrenches and sockets, and probably some pullers too. Anyone with a little mechanical sense and experience can restore one of these bikes.

What are the things that he or she needs to send out. What can't the typical amateur restorer do?

Well, they probably can't do the paint, there are only a few people who can do a really nice paint job. The other thing is the engine, it's unlikely they want to do the engine themselves, but they can easily send it out to someone who's a reputable engine rebuilder. I think the rest of it is doable. The motor and paint are the two big deals.

How do they get paint of the right color?

If you want a good color match, go to Don Hutchinson, or talk to John Healy.

Do you have to decide before starting the re-assembly whether or not you're going to ride the bike?

That would be a good idea. You can build it two ways, either make a rider out of it, or make it museum quality. If you make it museum quality, you probably don't want to go out and ride it. For most people, after spending a lot of money on a real meticulous restoration you probably don't want to put a lot of miles on that same bike. Most of the Triumph people I know are serious collectors. None of them have any intention of riding the bike.

What are the things that separate a good restoration from a half-assed attempt.

One good thing is having a good source of parts, there is some aftermarket stuff that's good, some is crap, you need to buy the correct parts.

If I'm restoring a Triumph with the intent of winning shows, what does that take?

If it's a show bike, you are talking museum quality again. To start with, this requires a really good paint job. It needs to be nicely applied and it needs to be the right color. Then be sure the person who does the motor does a really nice job. It should look just like it did when it left the factory. Once it's

together, do a good detail job on the bike. By that I mean make sure all the fasteners and all the hardware are correct.

Be sure you have all the right nuts and bolts and lock washers, all the correct fasteners. All the parts that were originally cad plated need fresh, cad plating. You simply have to be sure you get everything exactly right.

What are the mistakes people make when they do a restoration, where do they fail?

People don't find a source for good hardware. For example, they can't find the original Wentworth or CEI stuff, they go to the hardware store and use those fasteners instead, and it just isn't right. Hardware, including fasteners, is a big deal. Finding the right hardware can be as hard as finding the right sheet metal. Things like the right shock bolts and the engine bolts, that's where people make their mistakes.

Sometimes a person will mean well and have good intentions at the beginning of the project. Then the pocket book starts to get thin and they finish it up with cheap parts. Those cheap parts will spoil the whole bike.

How about the seat, where can I get the right seat?

It is virtually impossible to find a NOS seat in excellent condition. But you can go to a good seat source, they do some very good stuff. John Healy is one, British Cycle Supply in Canada is another. And there's JRC in California.

If you have a good seat pan, but you need chrome and a cover, John Healy or one of the others can take care of that. John will foam and cover it for you. But he won't paint the pan, you have to do that before you send it to him.

What about tires, can I still buy the original Dunlops?

A lot of these bikes used a Dunlop K7, but those made-in-UK tires are no longer available. The replacements are Japanese and they are exactly the same as the Dunlop. Some of the others are hard to find too, like the old original high speed Dunlop for the front. Sometimes people use an Avon Speed Master instead.

Chapter Two

Engine & Tranny Assembly

The '56 TR6 Engine goes Together

While overhauling a truly old Triumph twin at home might seem intimidating, Garry Chitwood reports that it's not as tough as it might seem. "Anyone who's done a unit engine can certainly build one of these. And I always tell people that a person with some solid mechanical experience can probably overhaul a unit 650cc Triumph engine."

"You need a good basic set of tools, also some Wentworth wrenches and some pullers. If you look at the photos, you see I don't use a ring compressor. That's an old-school trick. The person doing one of these for the first time, though, will

When we are finished with an engine, it is as close to new as we can manage. Even the cast aluminum parts look like they're brand new.

probably want a ring compressor designed for motorcycles - where the cylinder comes down from above the piston. Really, it's a matter of personal preference whether you use a compressor."

"As a general rule, the engine will be pretty grimy when you pull it out. I like to get it out, clean it if it's dirty, and then begin taking it apart. It's important to lay it all out the way you will put it back together. Inspect each part as you do the disassembly, again when you clean them, and one final time when you assemble it, to make sure all the parts are OK."

"There aren't very many differences between a unit and a pre-unit engine. Like I said, 'Anyone who has done a unit engine, can do a pre-unit, there are lots of similarities.'"

"I like to build the lower end of the engine, from the cylinders to the lower end, and put that aside. Then, if it takes me two months to put the rest of the bike together, all the gaskets in that motor are seated and the sealers are cured. With the timing chest cover it's important that there are no nicks in the gasket surface. If that surface is beat up, you might want to run the cover across a surface plate to ensure a good seal. You will need a service manual if you're going to build the motor, just to get information like the torque specifications."

"As we mentioned in the last book, it's important to wash the cylinders with hot, soapy water before assembly so the metal filings left from boring and honing are flushed out. Then coat them well with fresh engine oil. Otherwise, assembling an engine is a matter of being very neat and having good attention to detail. If you're not sure about something, pick up the phone and call somebody who's done it before."

We start with the crank, ready to be thoroughly cleaned.

I'm cleaning out the oil passages in the crank, and the sludge trap, with solvent.

Parts like the crankcases and the magneto case are bead blasted before we do anything else.

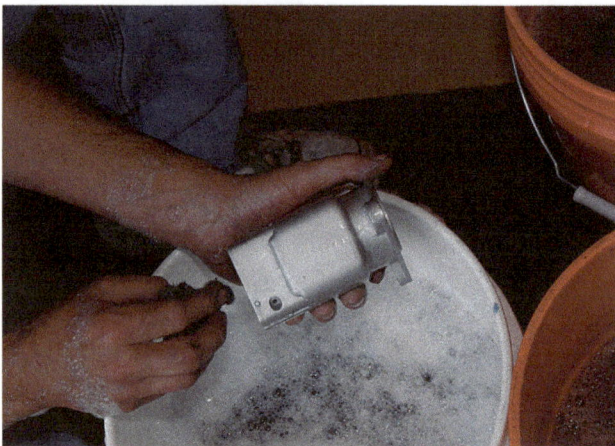

Next we clean the housings in hot, soapy water.

After being washed and rinsed, we put the parts in the oven at 350 degrees for ten minutes, this brings out the brightness.

The magneto housing, and all the other cast aluminum parts, looks like new after bead blasting, washing and drying in the oven.

The right side crankcase ready for assembly.

Before assembly I like to make sure the bearings fit the crank correctly.

The right side case with the bearing sitting just part way into the bore.

After the case is heated, we tap the bearing in with a hammer and a soft drift. I like to do this right after the cases have been in the oven at 350 for 10 minutes.

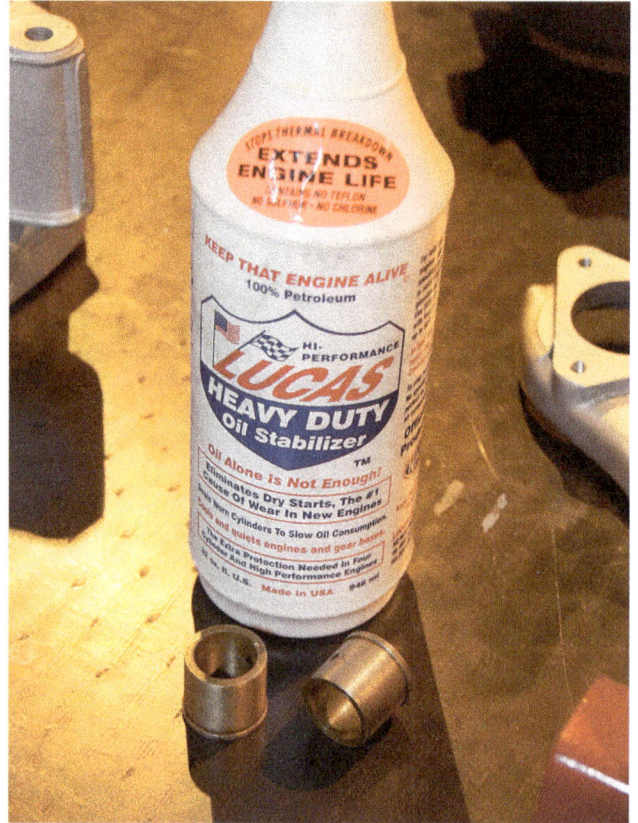

I like to put Lucas oil on the bushings before installation.

The right side cam (case) bushings.

After the case has been preheated, we tap in the cam bushings.

I'm using a tapered reamer to clean up any burrs on the cam bushings.

Here I'm using a hammer and punch to install the cam key on the intake cam.

We are going to install number 3134 intake and exhaust cams.

This is the cam wheel, I'm pointing out the timing mark.

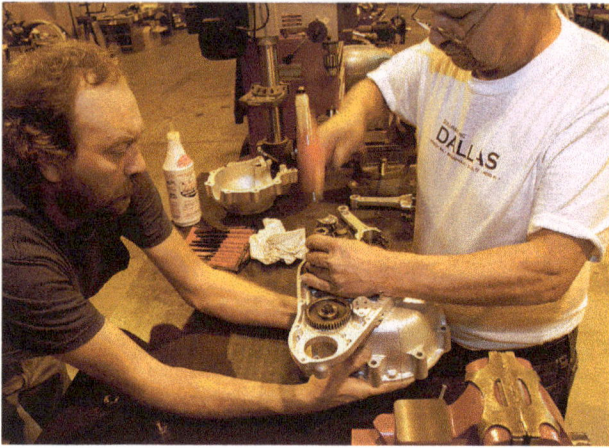

Installing the cam wheels for the camshafts.

The nuts secure the cam wheels to the cams.

Completed timing side chest with gears and cams.

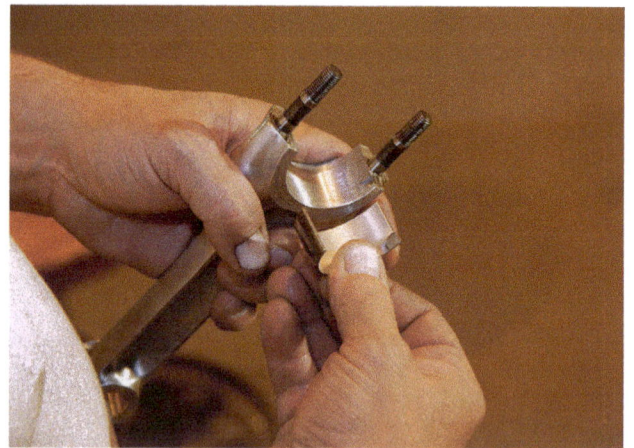

The new bearing insert is snapped into the upper half of the connecting rod.

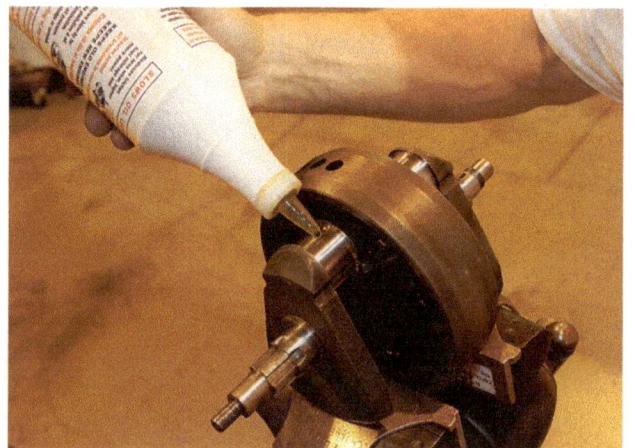

I'm using Lucas Oil for pre-lubing the journals on crank.

With rod bearings in place, I put on the bottom half rod cap, in the same position as before they were disassembled.

Now snug up the rod cap nuts...

I use a punch, as shown, on the rod cap nuts, to make sure they can't come loose.

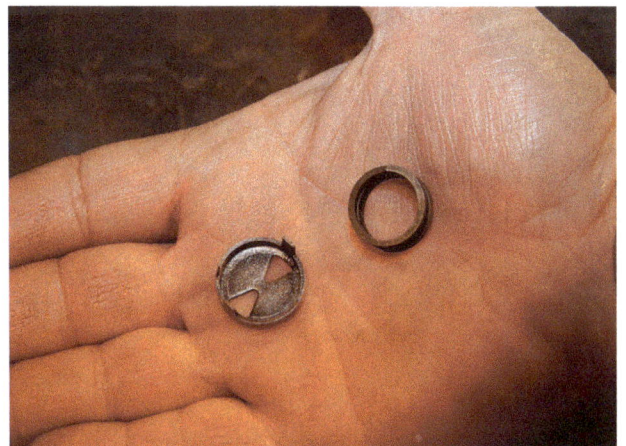

... and torque them down to 28 ft. lbs.

The breather spring ready for assembly into the left side case on the intake side.

Before assembly the cam bearings have to be pre-lubed.

Now we install the crank assembly into the left-side case.

Next, we apply gasket sealer to the left-side case.

Likewise, we put gasket sealer on the right-side case.

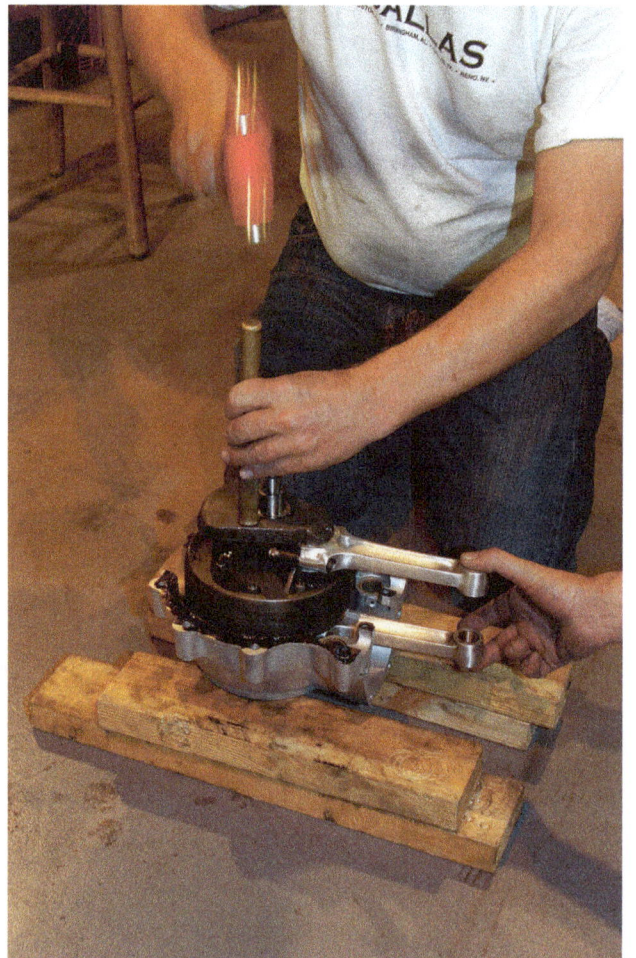

Using a brass drift and hammer, I lightly tap the crank down into the case.

Time to put on the other case half.

If everything is lined up OK, tap down the right-side case as shown using a rubber mallet.

Once the left and right case halves are together, it's a good idea to check for proper alignment, I like to rotate the crank to be sure nothing is binding.

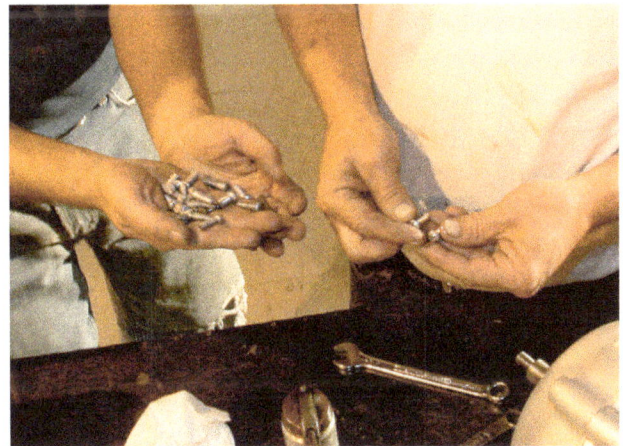

We are lucky to have a supply of the correct fasteners, so we're sure to use exactly the right bolt and nut on the case halves.

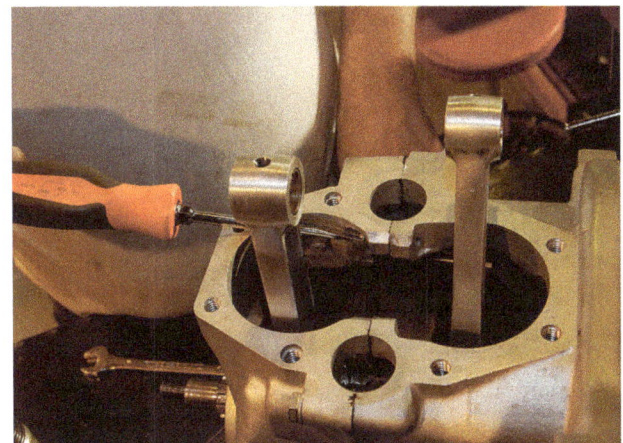

When you screw the cases together, don't forget these smaller fasteners.

19

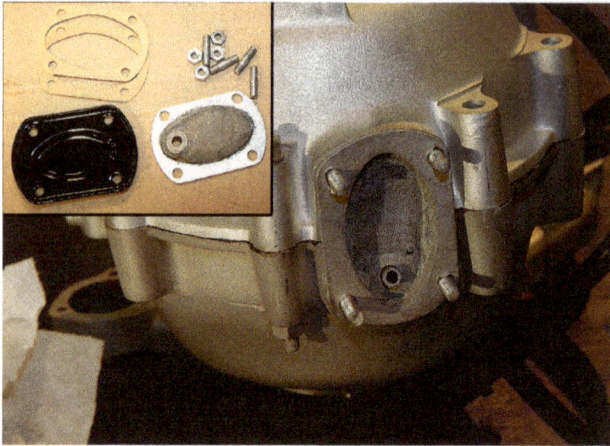

The gaskets in place, now ready for filter cover. Inset photo: filter cover, crank case oil filter, gasket studs and nuts.

We use lacquer thinner to wipe off excess gasket sealer, and keep the appearance neat and clean.

Filter cover being pushed onto crank cases.

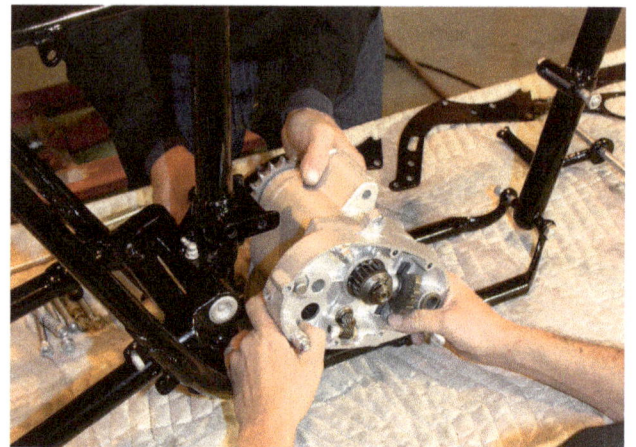

With the frame assembled we can install the transmission. Note: bottom stud for transmission is pushed out and ready to be put back in.

With the transmission in place, we can set the left side engine/transmission brace in place.

The transmission is in place, now we can set the bottom end of the engine into the frame.

Some of the through-bolts for the engine cases don't go into place until now. At this point it's nice to have an extra set of hands.

Next, we put the right side engine/transmission brace in place.

The studs shown here attach the rear of the engine/transmission braces to the frame.

Installing all the studs and nuts to mount the engine and transmission in a pre-unit is time consuming. Here we're installing the stud for the upper and lower frame connection.

21

We're installing the front-engine braces...

Close up shows the hardware in place for left and right front-engine brace.

...with the left and right front-engine brace in position we can insert the through-case engine studs.

The top two studs are in place, we are now moving down the engine case, installing the rest of the studs.

This is the distance tube used between the rear engine braces on bottom.

With the gearbox top stud in place, we install the gear box adjuster eyebolt.

The motor and transmission finally installed in the frame.

The eyebolt installed, you can see how it's used to adjust the tension of the primary chain.

Picture of gearbox adjuster, eyebolt and hardware.

Picture of intermediate wheel/timing pinion, and intermediate wheel spindle with nut and key.

The pinion gear is installed on the right side of the crank.

The nut shown here holds the pinion gear on.

Installing the spindle for the intermediate wheel.

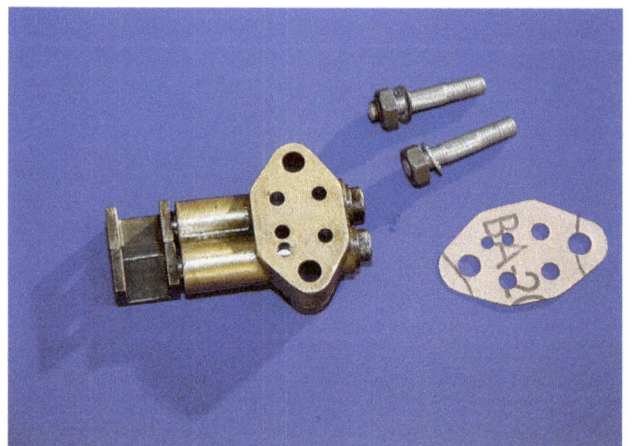

Use a new gasket, and the studs as shown, to install the oil pump.

With cams in place, install the intermediate wheel. Note the way we've lined up all dots marked on the pinion gear, intermediate wheel and timing pinion gear.

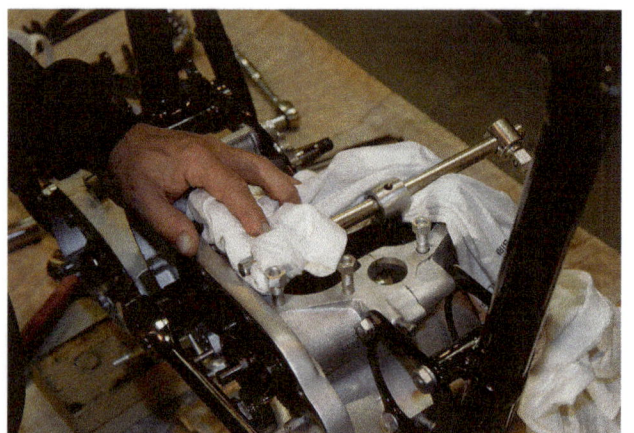

Tightening down pinion gear nuts and timing gear. Note: The left and right cam gear are left-hand thread and the pinion gear is a right-hand thread.

I like to pre-lube the oil pump before installation.

With the oil pump complete, and the gasket and studs in place, it's time to install the oil pump.

This is the drive block for the oil pump.

Here's the timing chest fully assembled.

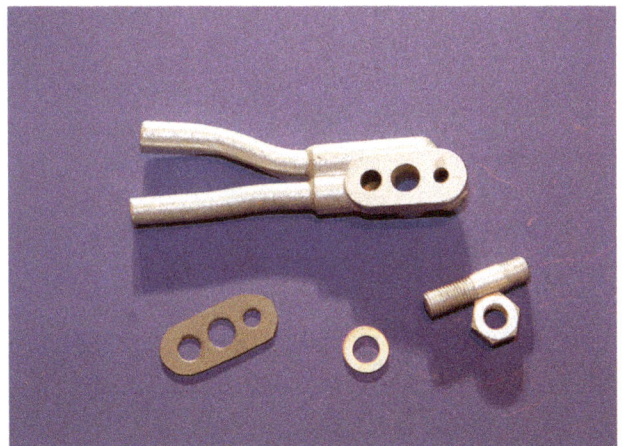

View of oil feed pipe, stud, gasket, nut and washer.

Installing the oil feed pipe to the crankcase.

Before installing each piston, the piston pin bushing needs to be pre-lubed.

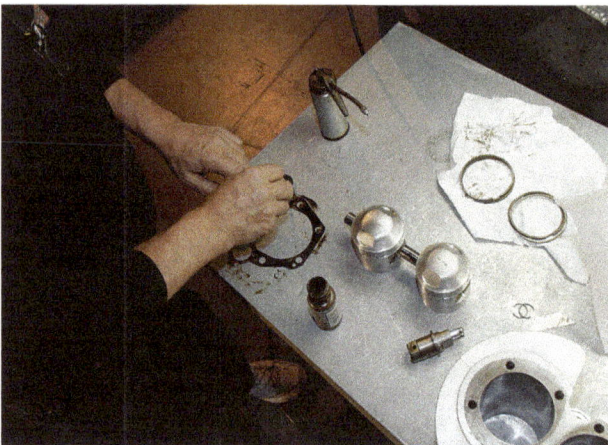

Before installing the top end, I spread sealer lightly onto the base gasket.

Once the pistons are in place, we install the circlips.

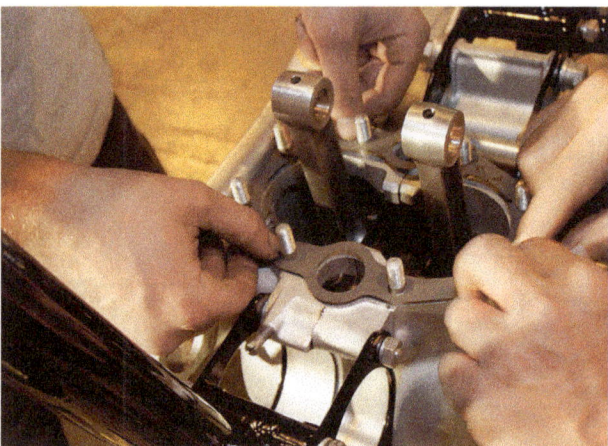

Next we set the base gasket onto the crankcase.

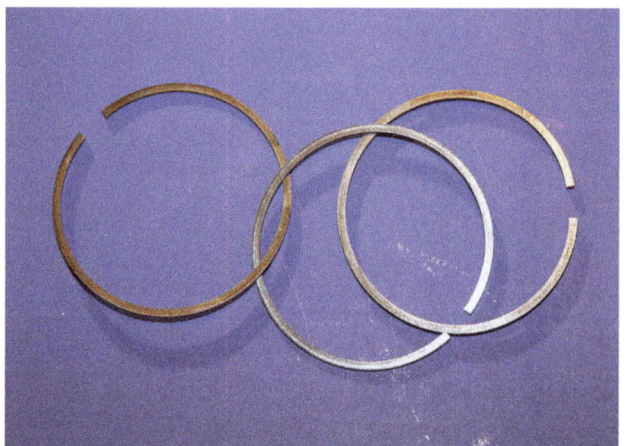

Piston rings are next.

I like to work the rings down the piston with care, rings are brittle and can break if you're not careful.

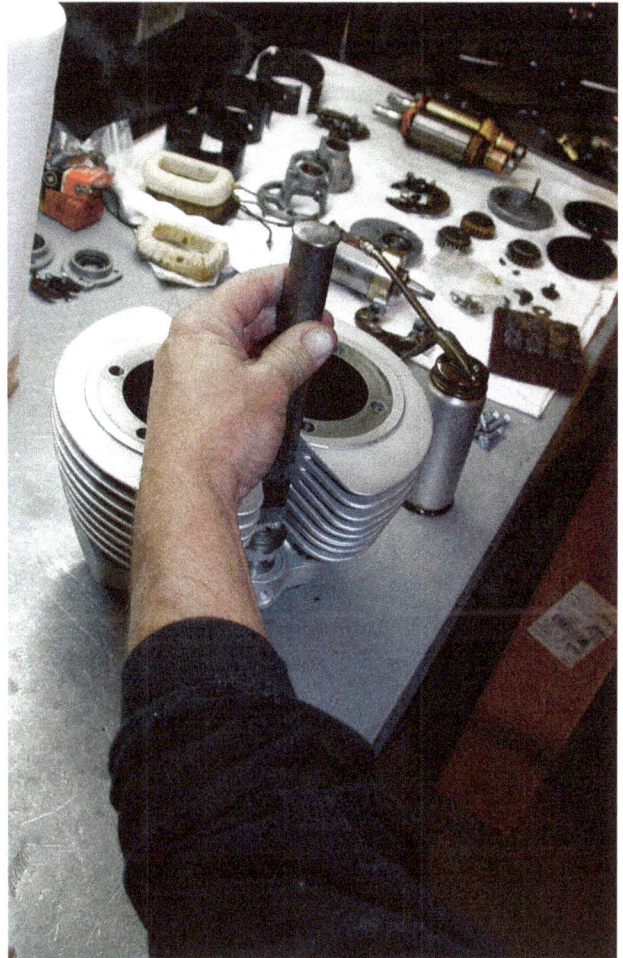

Triumphs use two guideblocks, each has two tappets.

We use a guide block tool to tap the guide block into the cylinder.

Installing the guide block, note the use of gray Permatex sealer.

With the guide block in place, we pre-lube the tappets before installation.

After tappets have been oiled, we push them into place in the guide block.

Positioning the rings on the piston for cylinder installation. Note: Ring gaps should be staggered and not lined up.

The tappet block screw locks the tappet block in place.

Note the plate that holds the pistons in place. We can now start the process of sliding the cylinders down over the pistons and rings.

Oiling up the left and right cylinder holes before sliding the cylinder down over the pistons.

Using "old school" methods, Garry squeezes the rings with two small screwdrivers and carefully...

It's a matter of pushing the cylinder lightly over the pistons. Don't force the cylinders down - BE GENTLE!

With the cylinder half way down, remove the piston plate from the engine case.

...works the cylinders down the piston. This is done one ring at a time, working from side to side.

With the cylinder installation almost finished, I take a rubber mallet and gently tap the cylinder the rest of the way down.

Cylinder Head
Assembly & Installation

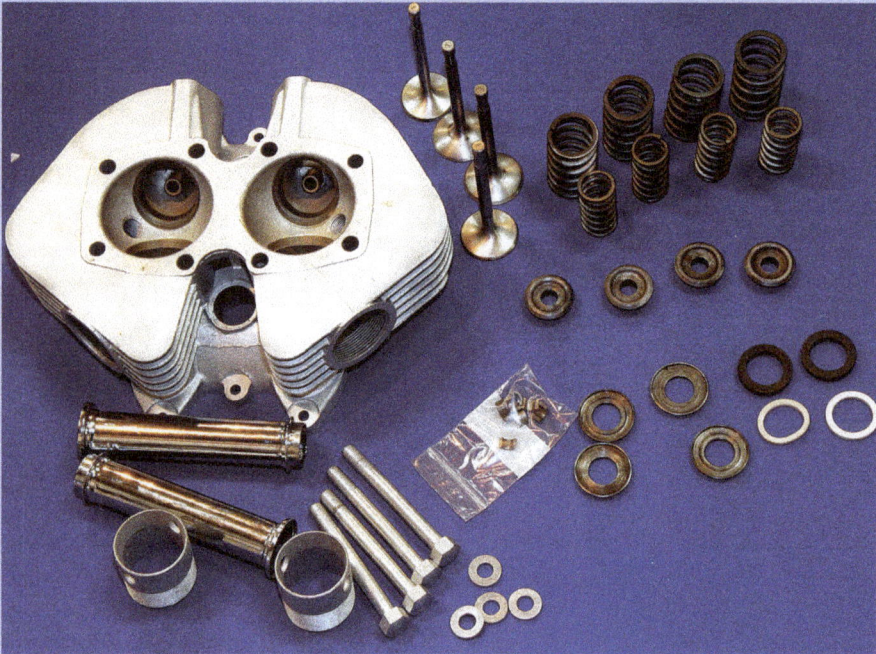

Some assembly required: cylinder head with spring kit and valves.

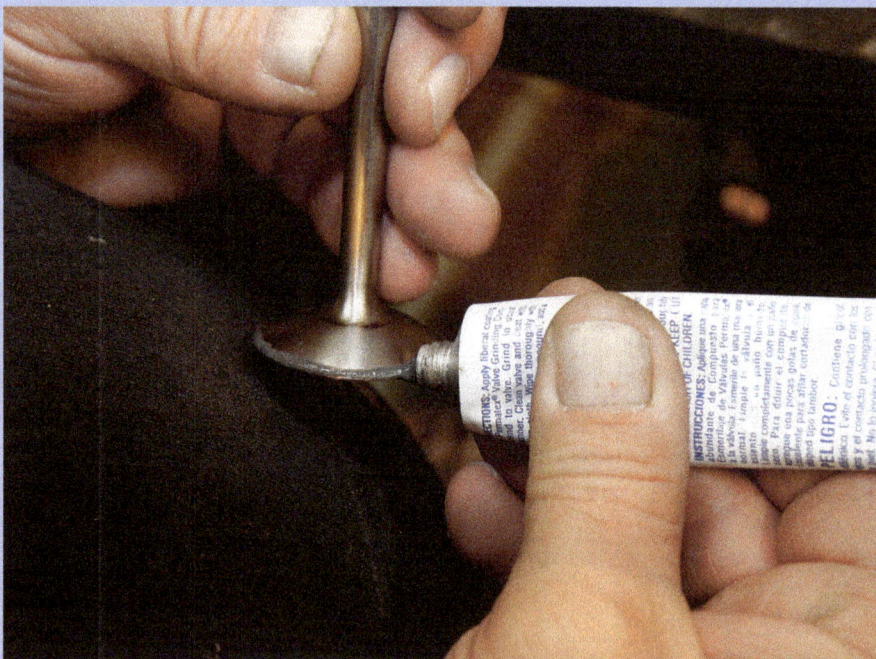

We put a light coat of valve grinding compound on the valve...

When you disassemble a Triumph cylinder head, there are a few key things to keep in mind. "The spark plug holes are often stripped, or the threads are at least in pretty bad condition," according to Garry.

"Now you need a heli-coil. And I recommend that you take the head to a machine shop, so the heli-coil is installed correctly. The other thing we see on a lot of these heads are stripped threads where the rocker box bolts on. There are four bolts that screw into the head and they're often stripped. Now you have to heli-coil those too."

"Sometimes the combustion chamber is beat up too, because something got in there and bounced around and did a lot of damage. And when people do valve jobs, they often cut the seats too deep. To fix that you will need to recut the seat and use an oversize valve."

"These earlier heads don't have as much trouble with cracking as the later ones did. You might however, want to resurface the head so there's a nice sealing surface. Too often that gasket surface is nicked up because people pried the head off the cylinders with a big screwdriver or pry bar.

...then slide it into the guide...

...put the suction cup lapping tool on the valve and "lap the valve into its seat."

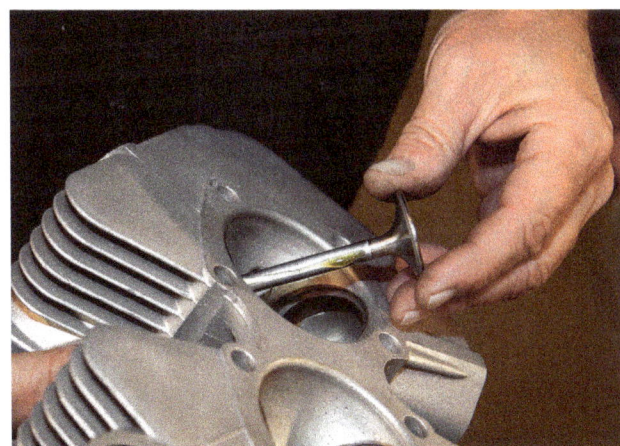

Now we drop on the inner and outer valve spring over the valve stem.

Once I'm sure we have a good match between the valve and the seat, all the compound is cleaned off, the valve is pre-lubed and slipped into the guide.

Next, I drop the top collar in place on top of the springs and use the valve spring tool to compress the springs.

With valve spring compressed I slide the two valve keepers into place on the valve stem.

Installing the spigot to the cylinder head on the exhaust side.

As shown, a complete valve assembly for the exhaust side.

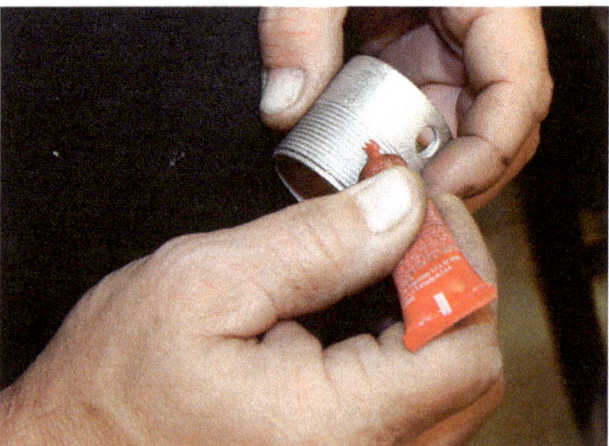

We like to put red Loctite on the exhaust spigot before installation.

I use a tapered punch, as shown, to tighten the exhaust spigot.

This is our finished head, all four valves have been installed.

Close up shows the guide block, seal, and tappets.

To install the pushrod, push it down over the guide block onto the oil seal.

With pushrod tube in place put the flat oil seal washer onto the top of the pushrod tube.

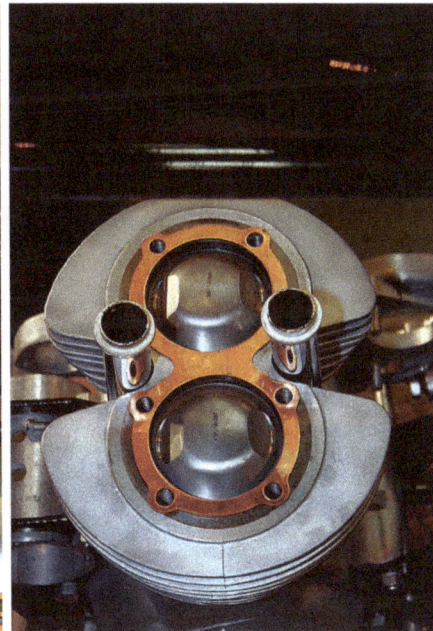

Here you can see the 2 flat white oil seals in place on top of the pushrod tubes, and the head gasket.

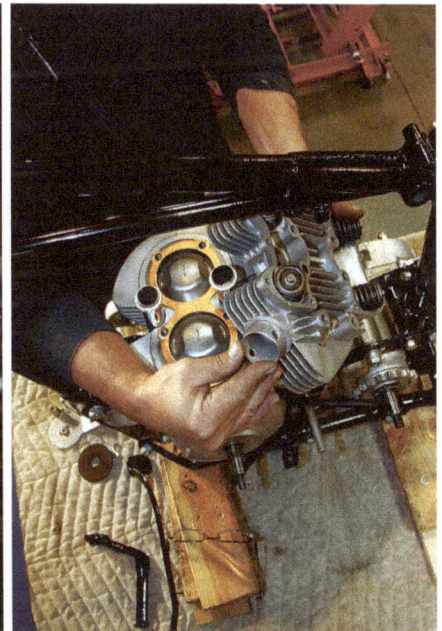

With the pushrod-tube seals and the head gasket positioned correctly, we can drop the cylinder head onto the engine.

With the cylinder head in place you can see the flat white seals squeezed between the tube and the head.

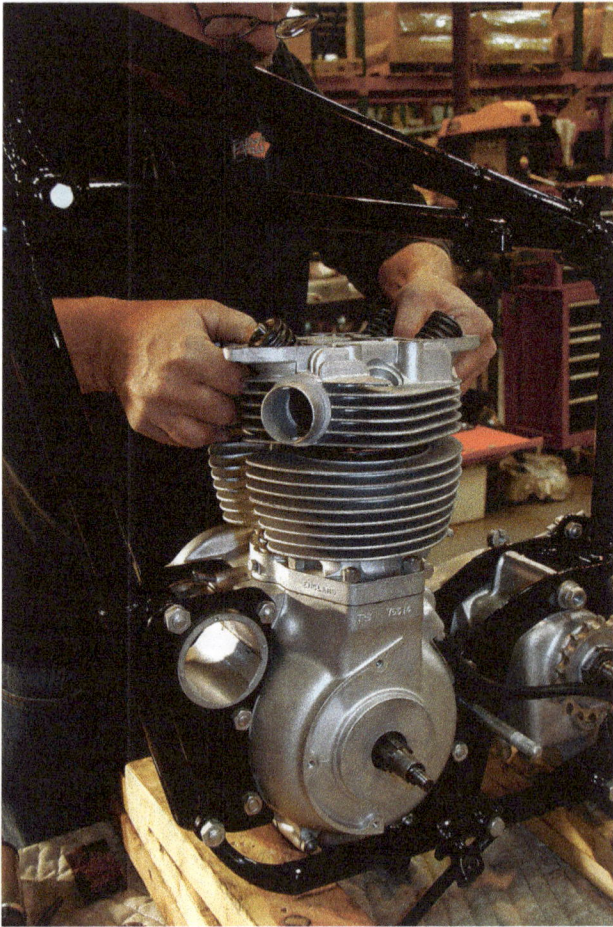

I like to be sure the pushrod tubes are mated up correctly with the head. Then I push the cylinder head down onto the cylinder.

After snugging down the head bolts, we torque each one down to 22 ft. lbs.

This is the nearly complete TR6C engine.

Interview - Garry Chitwood

Garry, how did you become involved in motorcycles?

When I was a young kid, the next-door neighbor had a '64 Bonnie and I used to wash it for him. I was about seven years old at the time. In about '70 or '71, I bought my first Triumph, a '64 TR6. This guy had a basket case and I bought it for 50 bucks. I just washed everything up, put rings in the motor, cleaned up the carbs, and took it down the street.

You did some racing too?

Yes, I had some Bultacos and Hondas and CZs before I stared actually racing, that was around '68 or so. Once I started racing I did motocross and flat track both. We would motocross on Saturday and Sunday, and flat track a Triumph on Friday nights, sometimes Saturday night too.

How did you learn your mechanical skills?

I went to work for Glenn Harden. He was a good machinist, taught machine shop and motorcycle mechanics. I used to help out in his shop as a young kid. I started for him when I was 15, working after school. He kind of took me under his wing as a young apprentice. Glenn had a really nice machine shop at his house and we would

Garry Chitwood, the man who's likely restored more Triumph motorcycles than anyone alive.

work there. We would fabricate parts, hone and bore cylinders, do anything that pertained to motorcycles.

How long did you work as a machinist?

I worked in that field 10 years.

When did you start restoring bikes?

I started ripping them apart in '78 or '79, but at first it was chopper stuff. In about '86 I started restoring. I had a friend who would restore old Chevys and I picked it up from him. After seeing what he did, the next time I took a Triumph all apart I put it back together as a restoration.

How did you learn to paint?

I just picked it up. I talked to some people and they showed me how to pull the trigger, and explained the importance of keeping a nice rhythm. But, basically I was self-taught.

What makes a really good restoration?

You have to have a special feel for it and really want to do it. You need some good skills, it's a lot more than just being a good mechanic. Seems like every bike you do, you do a little better. I always wanted to do everything, to do the machining, and the paint, the total restoration of the bike in-house.

How many hours do you spend on Triumphs now?

I run this warehouse for Bobby Sullivan and we have a small shop in the back. So when I get caught up on my warehouse duties I can work on bikes. And on weekends I always come down and work on motorcycles without any interruptions. It's nice, you can turn on the radio and just work on the bikes, there's nothing better than that.

How many restorations have you done?

Probably 230 or 240.

What do you see in the future, you and Bobby have been doing this for quite a few years now?

Lately we are doing more pre-units. I think though that as long as there are Triumphs out there that Bobby Sullivan and Garry Chitwood will be restoring them.

Transmission Assembly

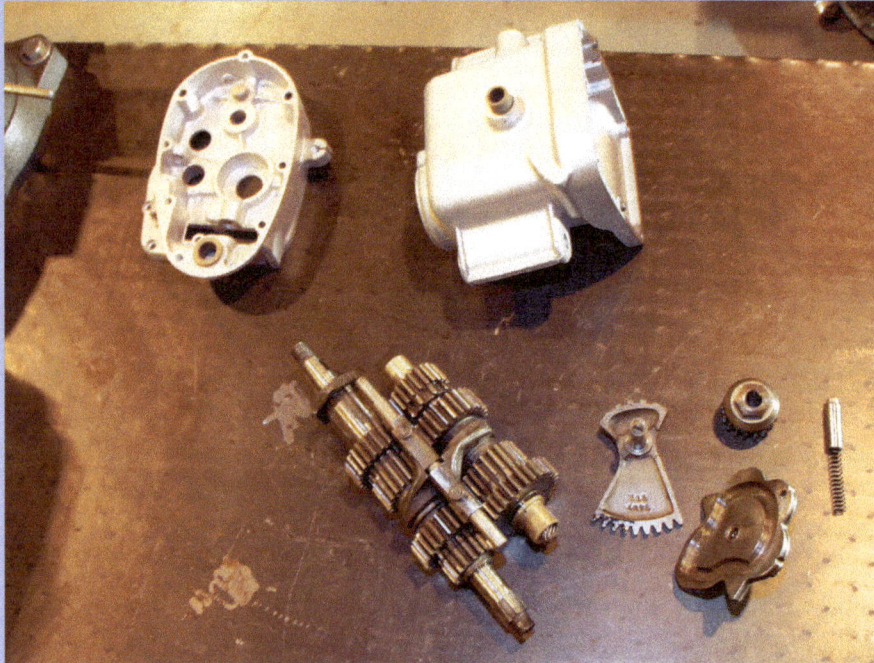

The transmission case and internal components prior to assembly.

Using a torch, we heat up the gear box case before installing the high-gear bearing.

If, according to Garry Chitwood, an engine is an engine, be it unit or pre-unit, the same thing can be said about servicing the pre-unit transmissions. As he explains, "A pre-unit transmission is like any other tranny. You have to be sure to inspect the shifting rods to be sure they are not bent. The other really important parts are the forks. Check them for excessive wear. Overhauling the transmission doesn't require any special tools, just your basic set from Sears, or Snap-on, or wherever. Like the engine, you should have a good service manual."

"Some pre-units use a needle bearing set to support the layshaft, but some use an oil-lite bushing on the inner cover and inside the case. These should be replaced, and they are still available. Once you put the transmission together, take the time to go through the shifting sequence to be sure it's shifting fine. I use Lucas oil for the pre-lube. It's pretty thick and helps to hold the gears together on the shafts. Once it's all together in the bike I fill the transmission with 80-90 gear lube."

"For gearing I like an 18 or 19 tooth sprocket on the counter shaft – the rear sprockets are all the same."

Once the case is hot, we set the bearing in place...

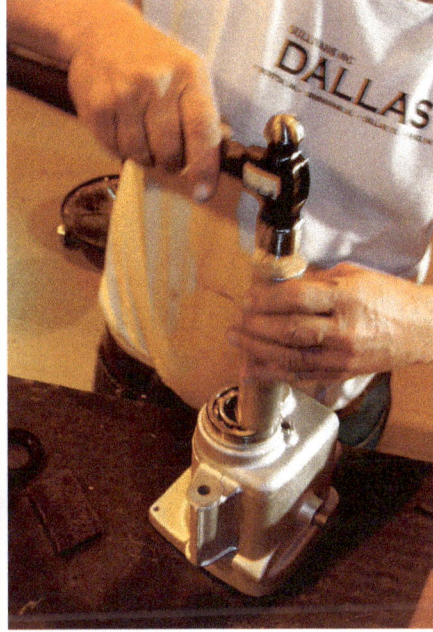

...and use a brass drift and hammer to lightly tap the bearing down into the gear box case.

We make sure the bearing is fully seated in the bore.

Once the bearing is seated we can install the snap ring.

With the circlip seated in the groove, we can install the oil seal.

Next we install the blanking disc into the gear box, I use a little Indian Head gasket shellac on the disc.

This is the lay shaft bushing ready for installation into the gear box.

With main shaft high gear in place, we can install the counter shaft sprocket.

I installed the bushing with a drift and a hammer.

Using the vice with a soft grip, we clamp down on the counter shaft sprocket gear and tighten the gearbox sprocket nut.

This is the main shaft high gear, and counter shaft sprocket.

Using Lucas Oil, I pre-lube the gear selector cam plate.

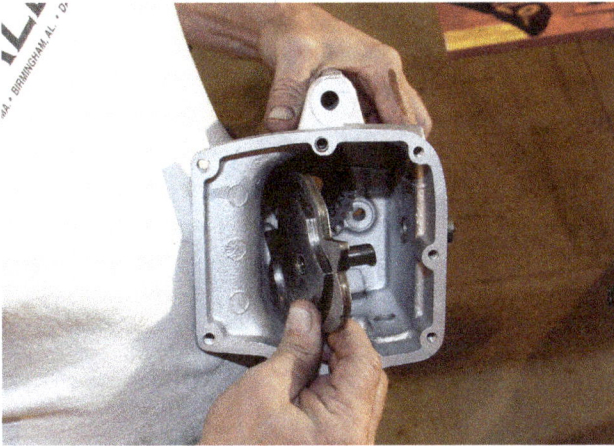

Now I can put the gear selector cam plate inside the gearbox.

Oil up the lay shaft for the gear box using Lucas Oil.

You can see the gear selector cam plate installed inside of the gearbox.

The layshaft needs to be pre-lubed before installation.

I put the whole transmission assembly together before installation.

With gearbox turned upright in the vice, install the complete gearset.

The transmission gearset is installed in the gear box, and I'm showing the position of the cam plate plunger.

As shown, index plunger is screwed into gearbox.

Here's the assembled gearbox.

The layshaft low gear needs to be installed on the bottom of the layshaft.

The inner transmission cover with layshaft bushing ready for installation.

1. Once again, the hammer and drift are used to install the layshaft bushing in the inner transmission cover.

2. The inner transmission cover and mainshaft bearing.

3. The inner cover needs to be heated, then the bearing can be easily installed with a hammer and drift.

4. With the main-shaft bearing in place, I can install the snap ring.

5. Time now to put in the cam plate operating quadrant.

Always check the fit of the quadrant spindle for the camplate operating quadrant, to insure smooth operation.

With camplate operating quadrant in place, install the quadrant spindle.

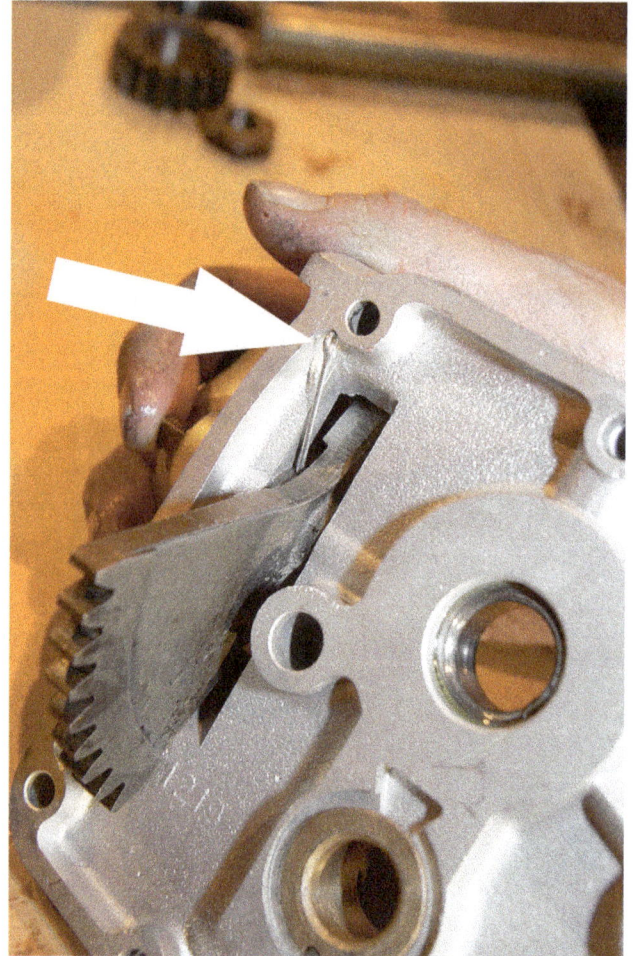

Installing split pin through camplate operating quadrant.

Speedo drive and bushing as shown.

I use a threaded shoulder nut for the speedo drive bushing installation (note the next photo).

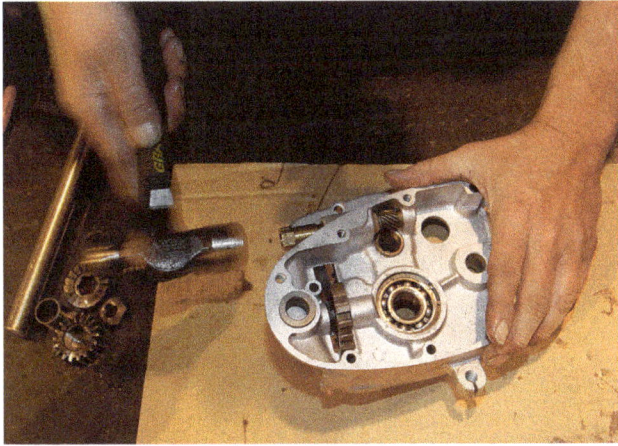

With the shoulder nut screwed onto the speedo bushing to protect the threads, we drive the speedo bushing into the inner transmission cover.

With the inner transmission cover 1/4 inch from the gearbox, line up the camplate operating quadrant as shown, dead center to spindle bushing.

I like to use gray, Permatex sealer on the inner transmission cover as shown.

Now I install the outer transmission studs to the inner gearbox.

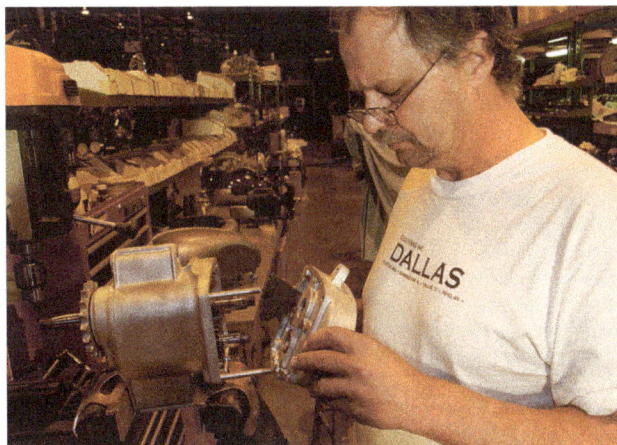

Now the inner transmission cover is ready to be installed onto the transmission gearbox.

Install the three inner cover screws as shown.

I tighten up the 3 inner transmission cover screws in two steps...

This is the kick start pinion gear assembly.

...finishing with an impact driver and hammer.

I start by installing the kick start pinion sleeve onto the mainshaft.

With both secured studs in place, I'm using a 5/16 inch spacer and 5/16-26 nut for sealing the inner transmission cover to the gearbox. Note: Remove nut and spacer before installing outer transmission cover.

Next, the pinion spring goes over the top of the pinion sleeve.

1. Install the kick start pinion spring over the top of pinion sleeve.

2. With the kick start pinion in place, install kick start ratchet to mainshaft.

3. The tabs shown here are bent over the nut to lock the nut in place.

4. The tab washer and mainshaft nut complete.

5. Don't forget to tighten the mainshaft nut.

Covers & Carburetors

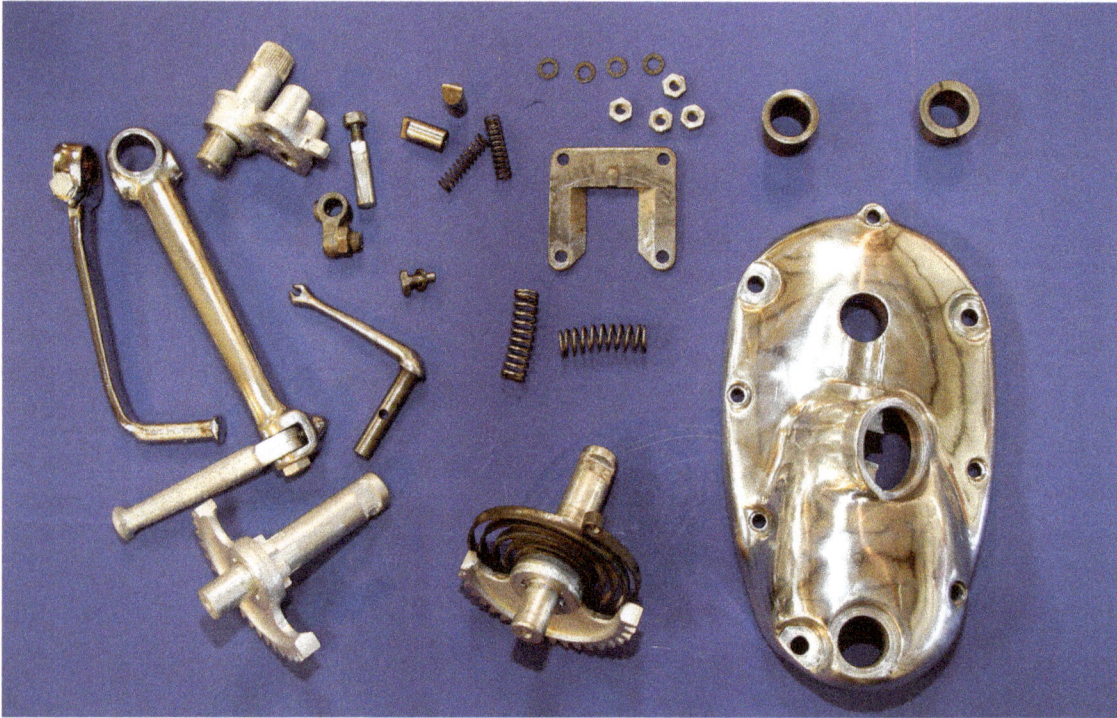

We like to spread out all the related components before beginning the assembly of a part like the outer cover.

Now we're installing the gear chain spindle bushing for the '56 TR6.

Using an alloy drift we tap in the gear chain spindle bushing.

With spindle bushing in place, install the gear change quadrant.

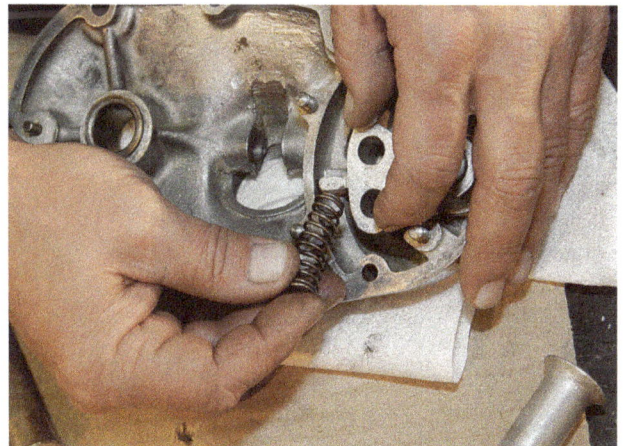

Now install the quadrant return springs.

Next we have to install the kick start spindle bushing in to the outer transmission cover.

Next, put the guide plate over the springs.

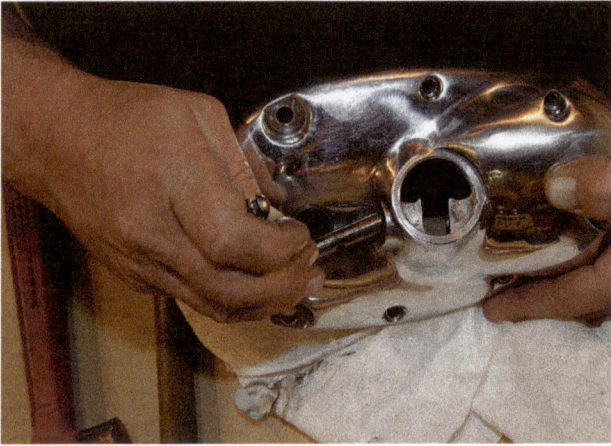

Install the clutch operating lever to the outer transmission cover.

Here's our nearly complete outer transmission cover, just a few more things to do before installation.

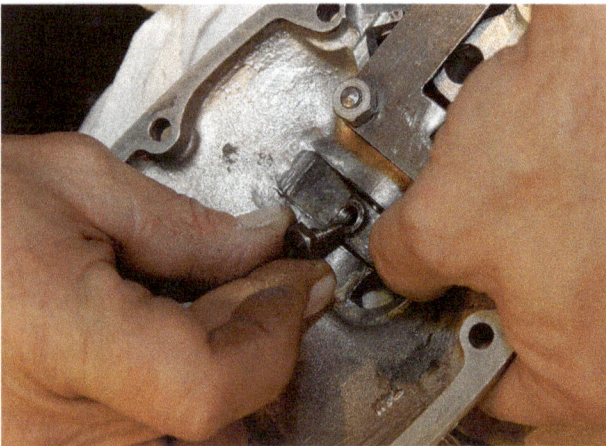

Next, we put the roller fixing pin in the clutch arm lever.

Now we put the kick starter axle in the outer transmission cover.

Installing the kick starter to kick starter axle shaft.

Install the locking bolt through the kick starter.

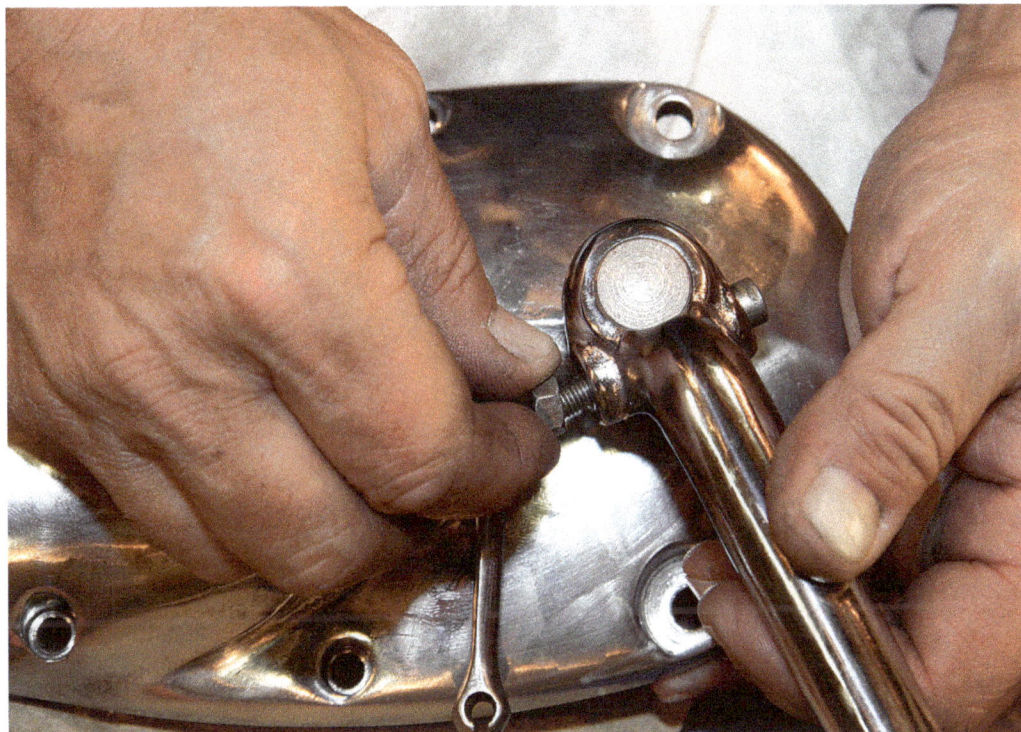

There are two gear change plungers with springs, install them as shown.

Finally, the complete outer transmission cover.

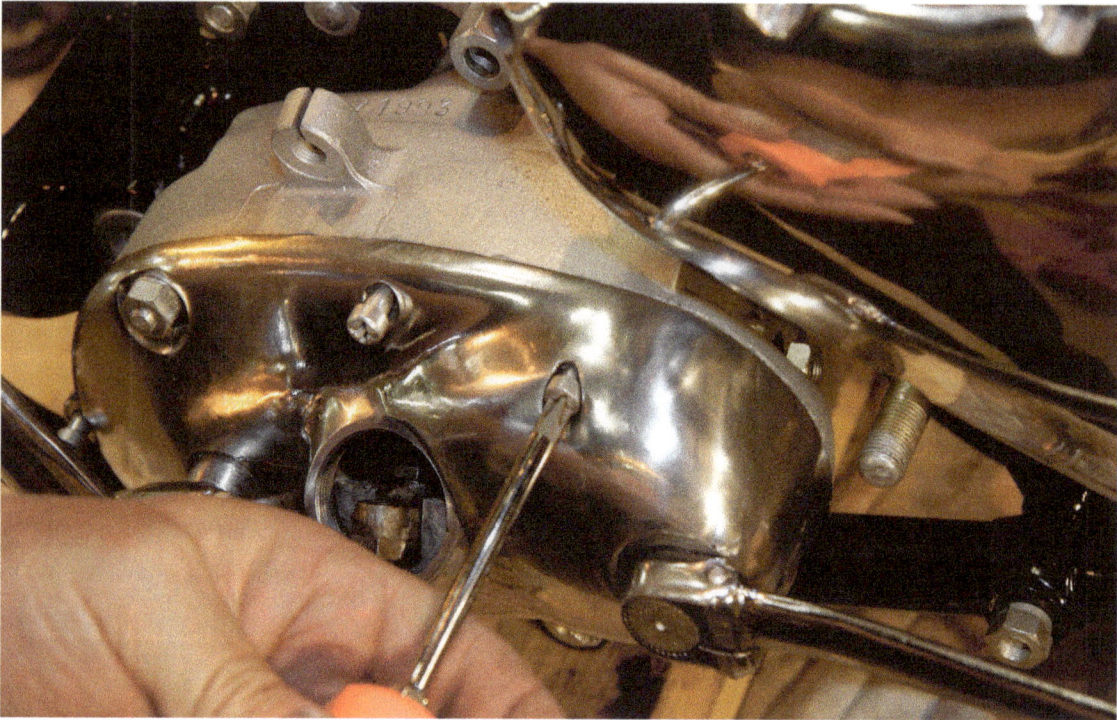

Now we can install the outer cover. Remember, these are not standard Phillips screw-heads.

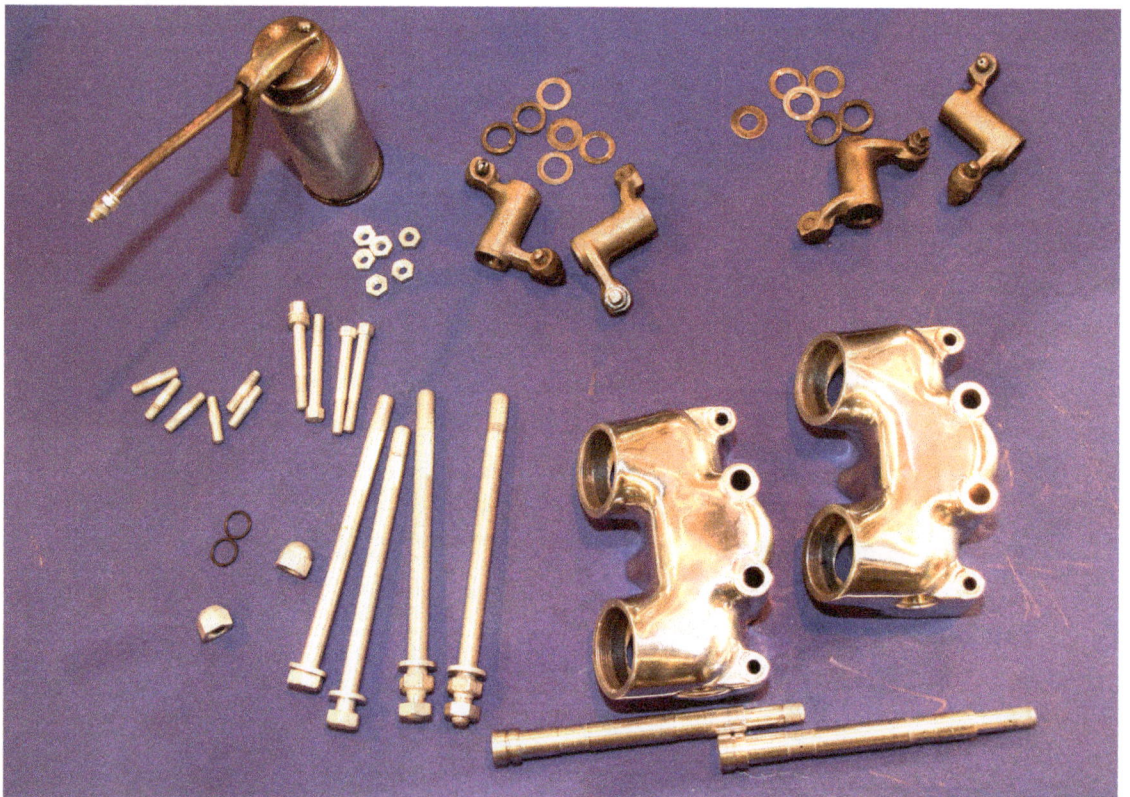

Shown are the rocker box assemblies, with rocker arms, shafts and all the hardware.

The rocker arms are supported on the outside by a washer and spring as shown. The washer goes up against the rocker, the spring is sandwiched between the washer and the rocker box.

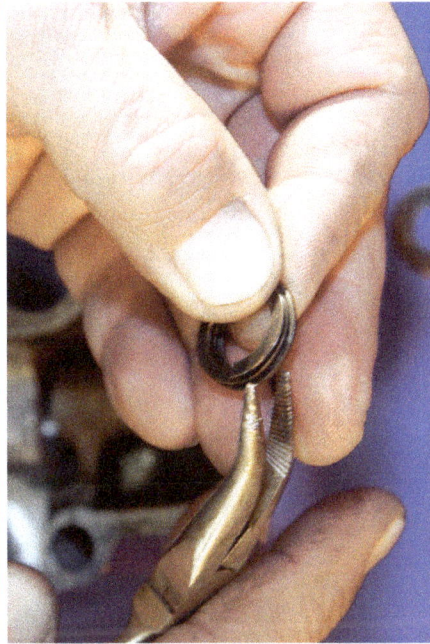

I use a needle-nose pliers as shown to compress the spring and washer...

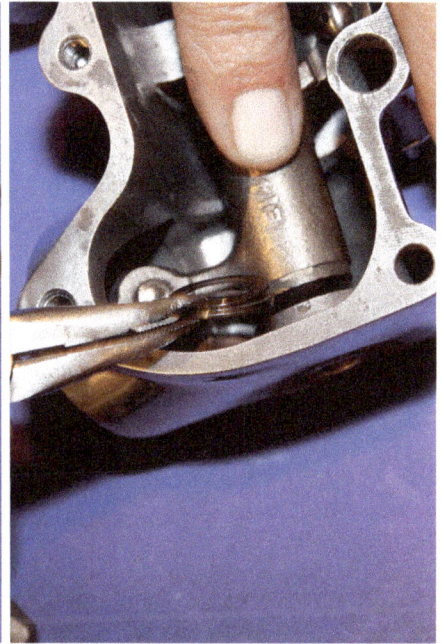

...and slip them into place as shown. Again, the washer should be positioned up against the rocker arm.

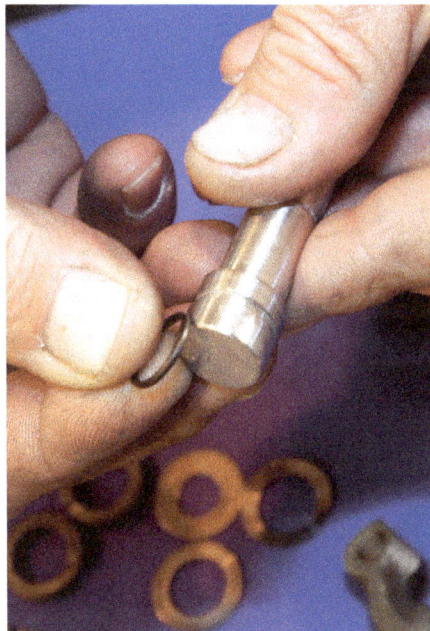

Be sure to install a new O-ring on the rocker shaft before sliding it through the rocker box. Pre-lube the shaft as well.

As shown, put the rocker in place, insert the outside spring and washer, then slip the rocker shaft part way up though the rocker arm. Now slip another washer between the rocker arm and center support.

The finished rocker box assembly should look like this. Starting at the very bottom of the photo we have: spring, washer, rocker arm, washer, support, washer, rocker arm, washer, spring.

51

1. Using a 30 weight oil, we pre-oil the bottom of the pushrod tube seats.

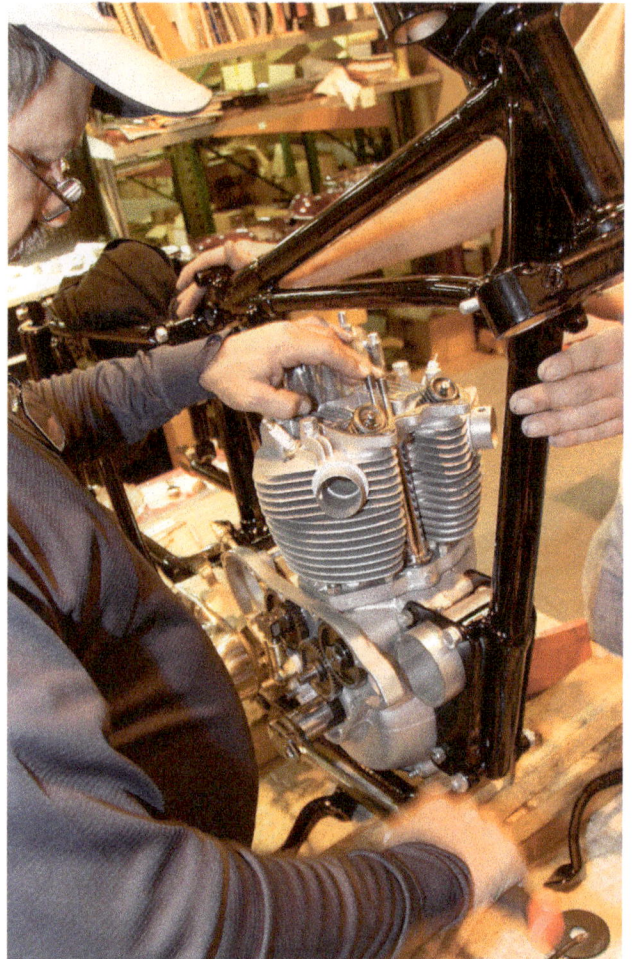

3. As a way to double check that the pushrods are seated, crank it over and make sure they move up and down.

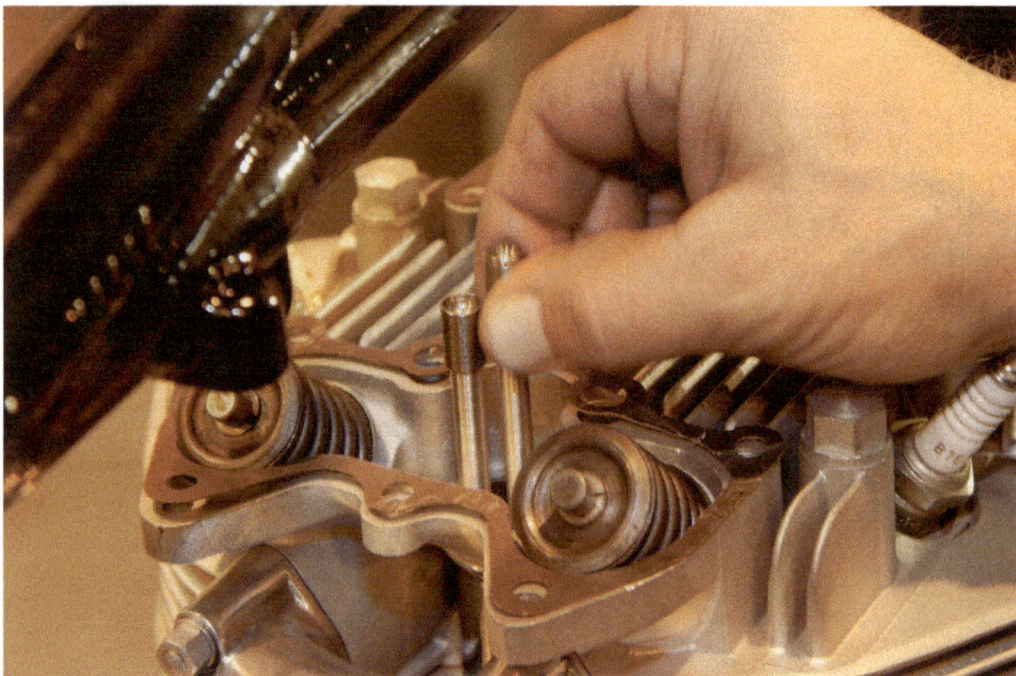

2. Install the pushrods into the pushrod tubes. The oil on the bottom of the pushrod seats will make it possible to push the pushrod down on to the tappet and then pull up slightly on the pushrod and feel whether or not it's seated on the tappet.

Set the rocker box assembly in place carefully, making sure the concave pushrods seat up against the dimple on the rocker arms.

1956 rocker box is shown bolted to the top of the head.

Set the clearance on the rocker arm to valve stem as shown, .002 inches for the intakes and .004 inches for the exhaust.

Tighten down the cylinder bolt heads with a torque wrench.

Using a feeler gauge, I check the clearance on the exhaust valve.

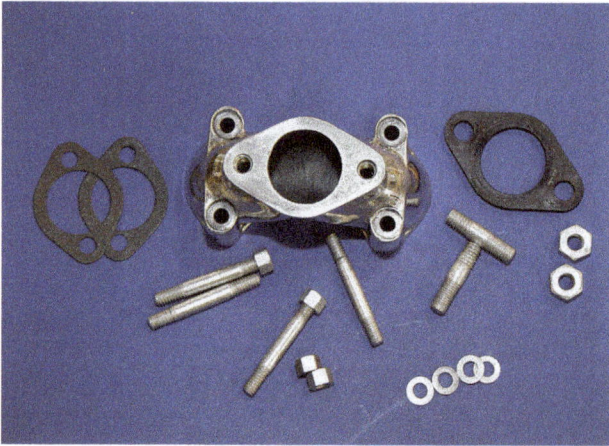

The intake manifold, gaskets and hardware laid out and ready for assembly.

Install the joint washer to the jet block.

Double nut the manifold studs for installation.

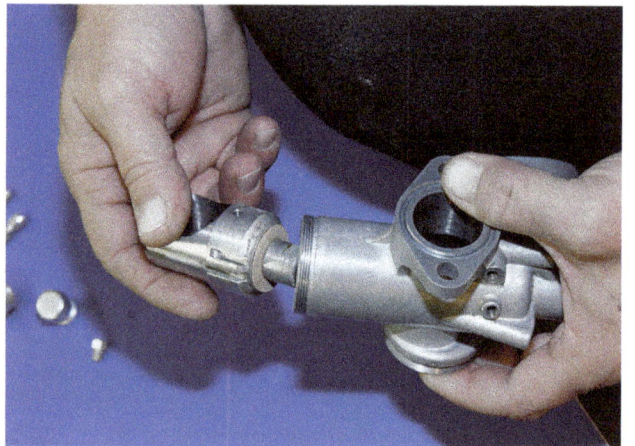

With joint washer in place, we now install the jet block into the carburetor.

A blow up of the monobloc carburetor and internal parts.

With the jet block in place, install the peg screw.

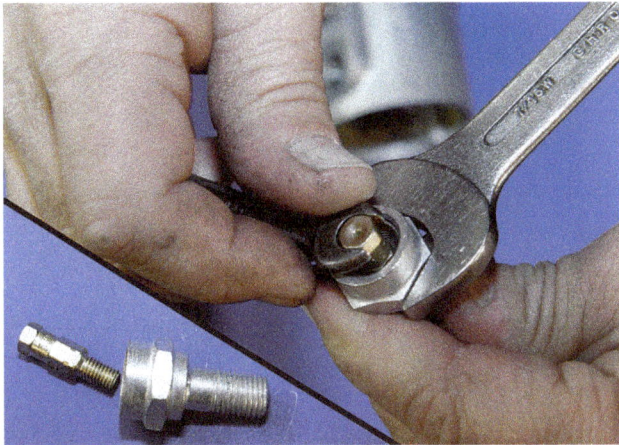

Install the main jet to the jet holder. Note: main jet is a number 250.

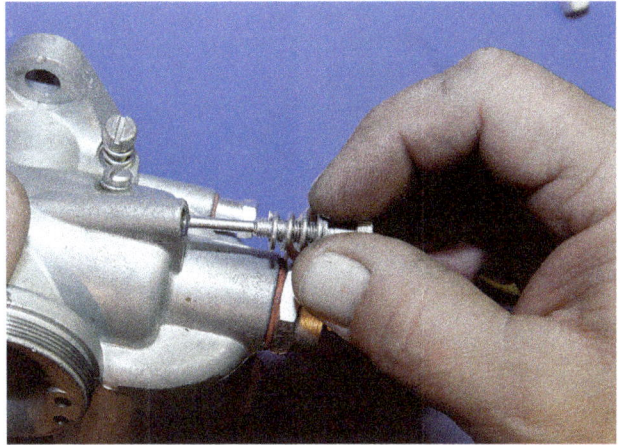

Now we install the throttle stop screw.

With the main jet in place, install the jet holder to bottom of the float bowl. Note the fiber-washer.

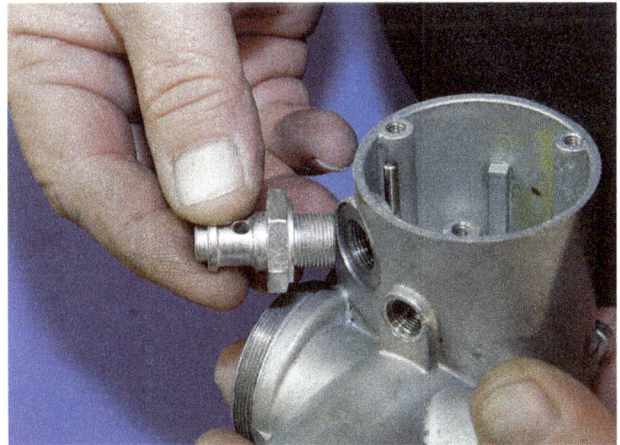

Install the needle seat in the carburetor bowl.

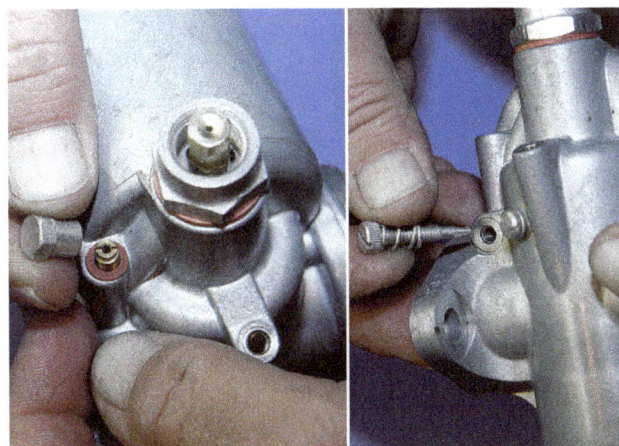

With a pilot jet number 25, we install the cover nut. Note: in the right-hand photo, I'm installing the air screw in the carburetor.

Now install the cover nut over the main jet.

The tickler spring and body assembly.

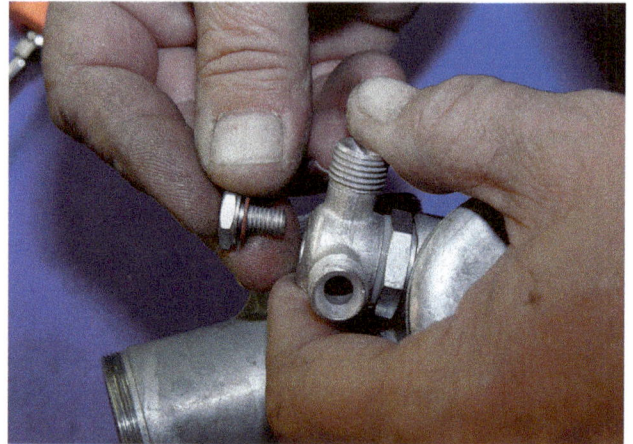

Now install the bolt to the pipe assembly.

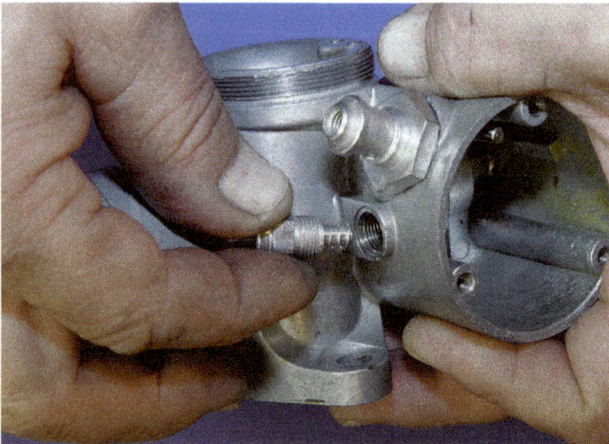

Install the tickler to the carburetor float bowl.

Next, install the needle jet to the jet holder.

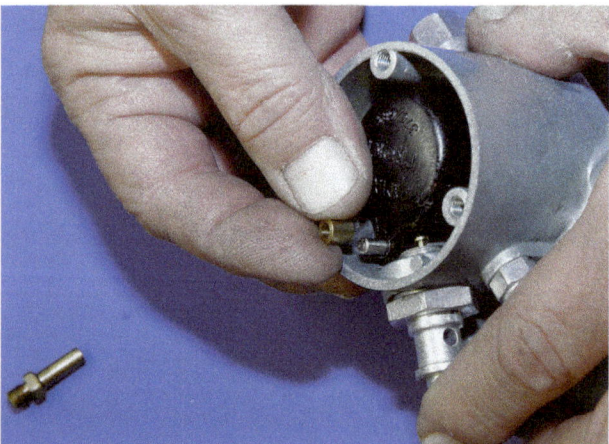

With the float bowl and needle in place, install the brass bushing distance piece.

The jet holder with the needle jet installed.

The complete air-valve assembly.

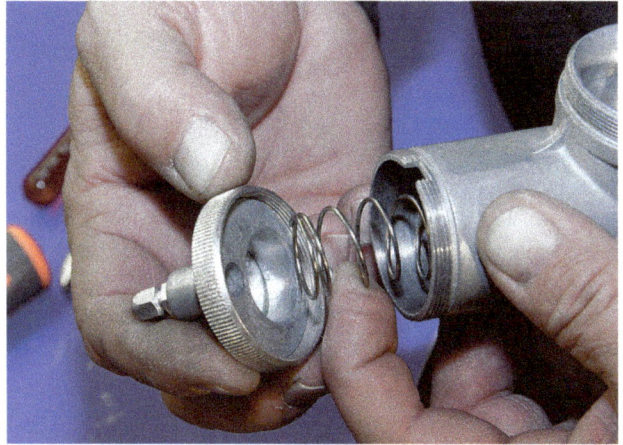

Return spring and cap ready for installation.

Throttle valve and needle as shown.

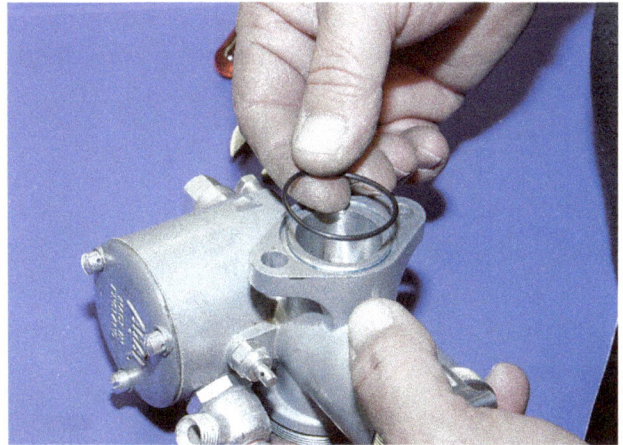

Install O ring to carburetor flange.

With the needle in place, install the throttle valve into the carburetor.

Viola, one complete rebuilt carburetor!

Chapter Three

Assemble & Restore a '56 TR6

From a Pile of Parts to a Complete Motorcycle

Not surprisingly, when Garry Chitwood starts on the assembly of a Triumph, he starts with the frame. "We have the frames powder coated these days," explains Garry. "And sometimes the shop doesn't cover the holes in the frame when they do the powder. So we run taps through any holes that are threaded to clean out any paint or powder coat."

Even before he starts prepping the frame though, Garry likes to lay everything out to make sure it's all there. "If you have the room, lay every piece of that bike on the bench or floor. Once you know you have ninety nine percent of the parts,

A finished and rare 1956 TR6. The difference between a really good restoration and an OK restoration is in the details. Read on to find out exactly what we mean.

then go ahead and start the assembly. By laying it all out like that, the engine parts in one area and the wheels in another, you can see exactly what you have and spot what you're missing. Now you can order any missing parts before you start. Some of the missing parts are items you don't need right away, but others will stop the whole assembly process. The important thing is to figure out what you're missing, decide when you need it and where you can find that missing piece. Laying the entire motorcycle out ahead of time is a definite plus."

"I always say, different strokes for different folks, but we put the rear frame section on, then the swing arm, and then we build and install the shocks. After all that we start the front end. Sometimes the forks are bent, So I always use new tubes. The same with bikes that use outer springs, I always replace the springs. If they're internal springs, I may or may not replace them depending on condition. You can get the new springs from either Mitch Klempf or John Healy. When we assemble the forks I always insist on new bushings and seals."

"After doing the frame, depending on the year, you can go ahead with the wheels. We always take the wheels apart, send the rims out to the chrome shop, powder coat the hubs, install new bearings, and send the spokes and hardware out to be cad plated. We have everything we need to assemble our own wheels, including a truing stand. You can buy a cheap truing stand for a couple of hundred bucks, or you can just clamp the axle in the vise (use soft-jaws on the vise) and do the truing that way."

"Next you want to start working on the motor and tranny, get the lower end of the engine and the tranny in the frame, because that is part of frame assembly. Just get it all sitting there, all the studs in place and the engine mounting plates in place loosely. Then follow the sequence we did with the '56 TR6 in this chapter.

"On pre-units you need to be cautious, if you don't follow the right sequence you will have to go back and unbolt something and then start over."

"The important thing is to have a plan and follow a sequence, that makes all the difference in the world."

Our 1956 TR6C before disassembly.

It's nice to have enough bench space that you can lay everything out ahead of time. 7921

We start the reassembly with the frame, shown here after powder coating.

The frame always needs some detail work before assembly can start, here I'm removing paint from a mounting hole.

With the swingarm and frame section aligned we can drive in the swing arm pin.

Sometimes we use a small disc grinder to remove powder coat off areas like the swingarm to ensure a proper fit.

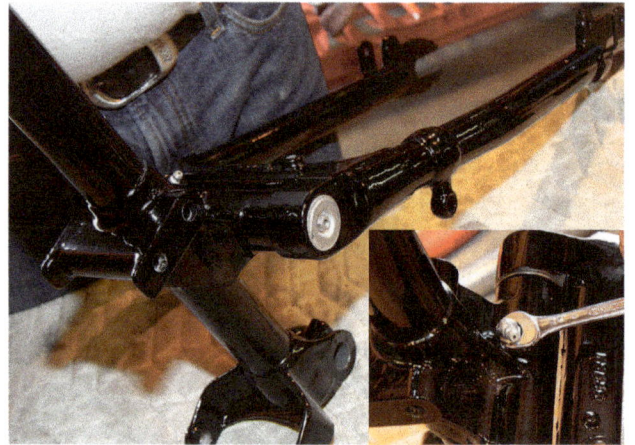

The swingarm with the pin already driven into the frame, note that we've added the grease caps.

With excess paint out of the way we can line up the swing arm to the rear section of the frame. Note, there is only one, 5mm, spacer used on the right side.

I'm adding the rear section to the front section of the frame. Note: Be sure the return spring link is installed at this time (inset photo).

It's a good idea to chase the threads on all the studs, and any holes taped into the frame.

Start the bearing race installation as shown with a brass hammer.

Finish the race installation using an alloy drift, tap lightly to install the race.

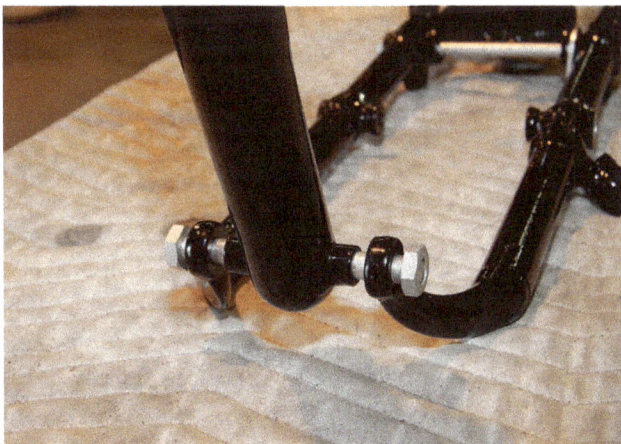

Here are the fasteners used where the down tube meets the front of the lower frame.

Before the assembly, collect the top and bottom triple tree, races and ball bearings.

After the races have been installed, grease the races prior to putting in the ball bearings.

After the lower tree and upper race are in place, installation of the top tree is next.

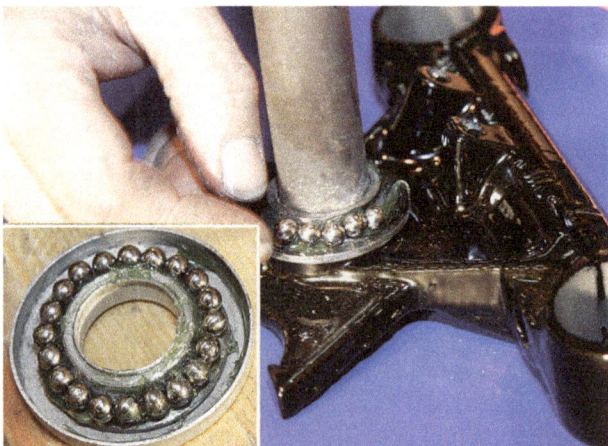

With the bearings and races in place, install the top and bottom triple tree. There should be 20, 1/4 inch ball bearings in each set.

We install the neck from the bottom, then carefully drop on the upper race and bearings as shown.

Next, tighten up the top fork stem sleeve nut until there is no play in the top or bottom lug.

With the shocks in place, we can put on the lifting handle.

With the engine in place we add the 2 engine torque stays.

With a little help from Danny, the rear fender is next.

Here I'm tightening up the front 2 bolts for the rear fender first.

With the left and right headlight ears in place, I can now put the fork tube through the top and bottom triple tree.

Danny holds the fork tube while I uses a block of wood, and a hammer, on the bottom of the fork tube to gently tap it into place.

Here's the fork tube completely pushed through the top and bottom triple tree.

The steering damper rod goes in as shown.

The damper rod connects to the friction disc and adjuster sleeve - installed on the bottom of the triple tree as shown.

Now install the locator pin for the adjuster sleeve.

Before assembly, be sure to wash the restrictor rods and springs in some kind of solvent.

These are the bearings for the lower legs.

The left and right lower leg for our TR6C.

Here I'm installing the restrictor rods in the right fork tube.

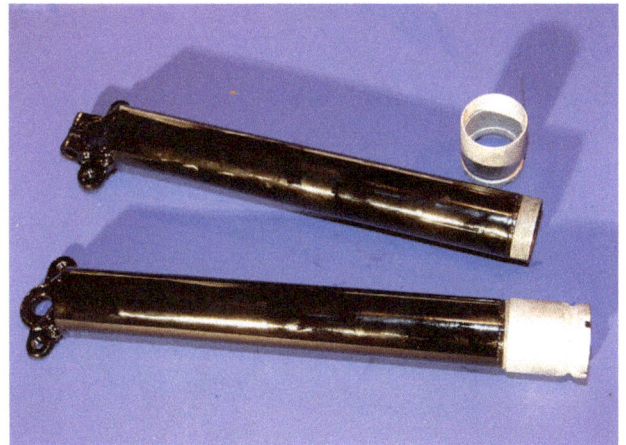

Assembly of the dust excluder sleeve nut starts with the plain washer as shown.

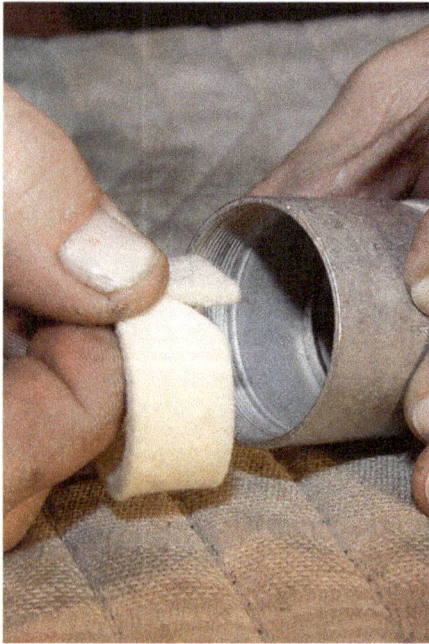

The next step is to insert the cut felt for the oil seal sleeve nut...

...followed by the second plain washer for the oil seal (the two washers are the same).

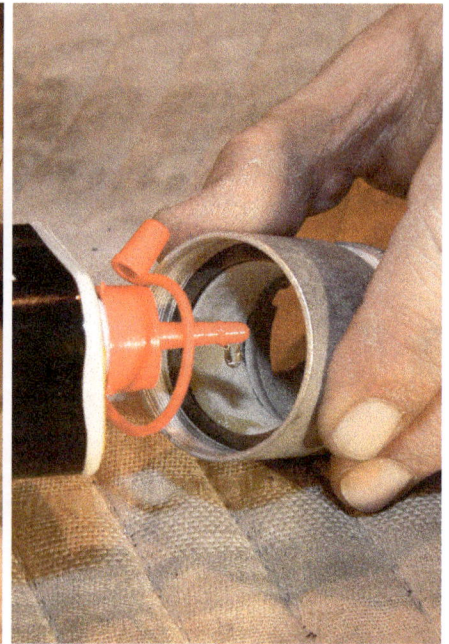

Now, using light oil, saturate the cut felt.

Here we slide the dust excluder sleeve nut over the restrictor rod...

...and install the lower bearing to the fork tube...

...followed by the sleeve nut for the lower bearing fork tube.

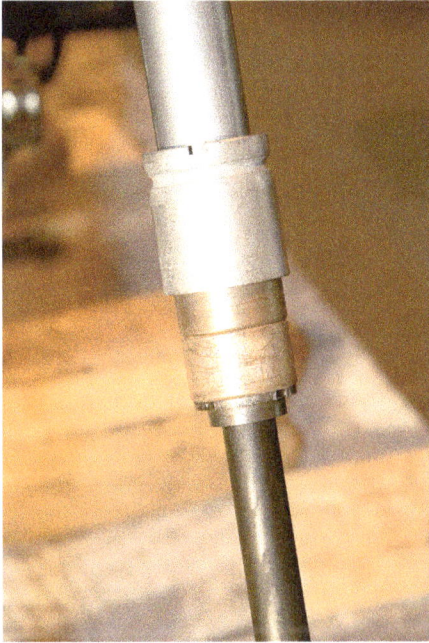

Dust excluder sleeve nut, bearing and restrictor rod.

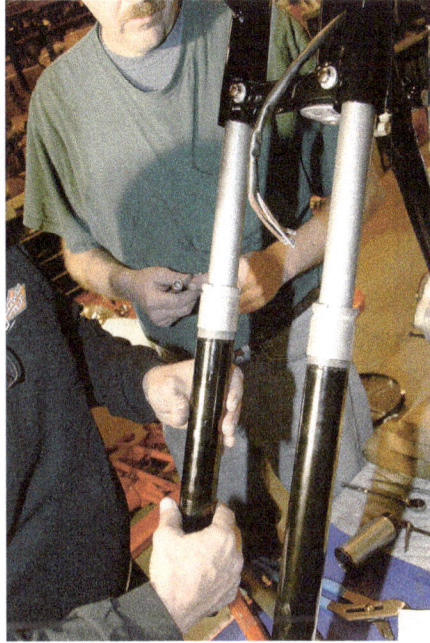

Install the fork legs by sliding them up into the fork tubes.

Screw the dust excluder sleeve nut over the fork tube.

Now put in the flange bolt for the restrictor tube.

Install the bottom gaiter clip to the dust excluder sleeve.

With the gaiter clip in place over the fork gaiter rubber, I can now tighten the clip counter clockwise.

Here I'm positioning the front fender.

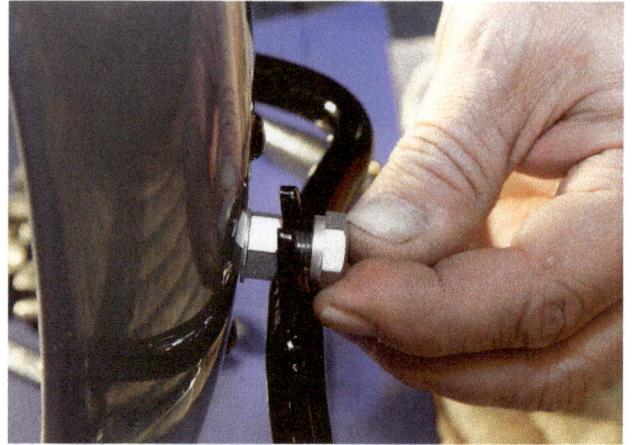

The front fender attached to the stay with a spigot nut. The threads are 5/16X26.

Garry is now putting on the front fender brace and 2, 1/4 inch bolts, with the top cap.

Install the one inch handlebar to the top tree.

Now we're adding the bottom stay for the front fender.

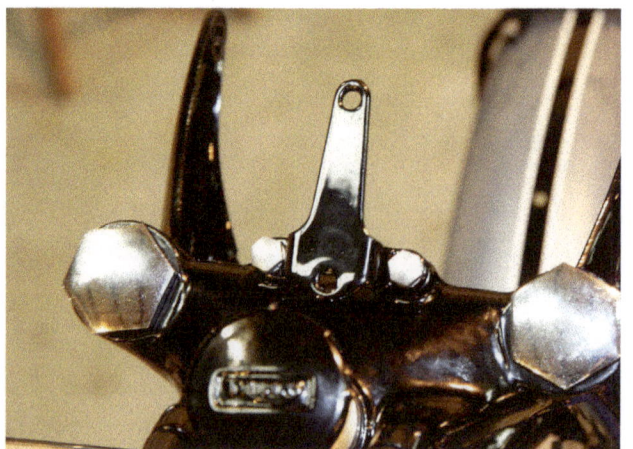

This bike uses a single gauge mount, mounted to the top tree as shown.

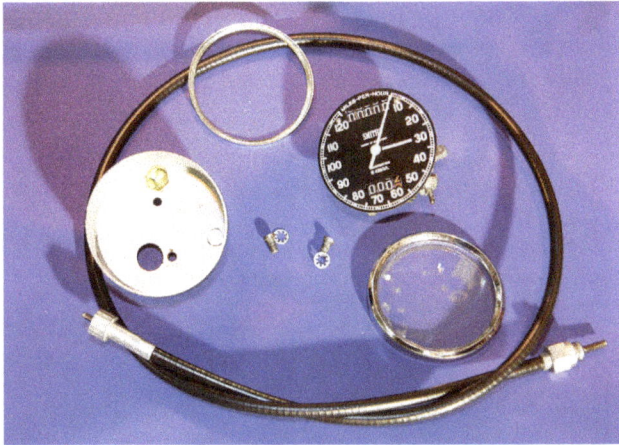

The 120 mph speedo waiting for assembly.

The brake assembly starts with installation of the front brake shoes on the front brake plate.

Once the shoes are in place, install the brake cam lever and nut.

The speedo assembled and installed on the 1956 TR6C.

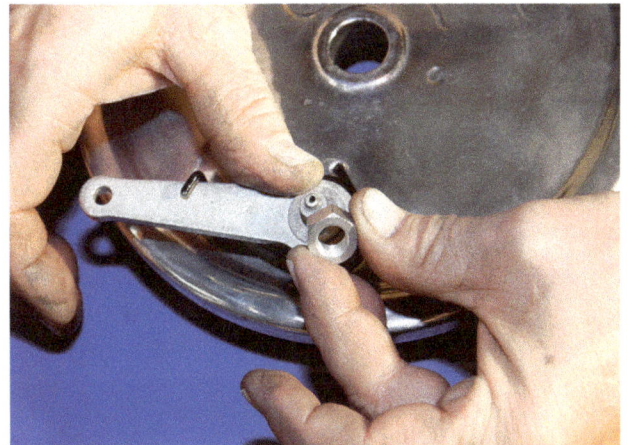

Now the brake plate and brake shoes are ready for installation to the front wheel.

With the front wheel complete we can slip it up between the fork legs.

Install the brake lever to the handle bars.

This is the front brake cable adjuster for the front wheel.

Install the dip switch and horn to clutch lever bracket.

The end of day 3 of the 1956 TR6C assembly.

Rear wheel with brake hub already mounted.

You have to measure the rear axle to ensure the threaded portion is the same dimension on each side.

Lay out of brake cover, brake shoes, lever arm and spring.

With the wheel and axle in place, install the axle adjusters on each side.

With the rear wheel assembly completed, James and I install the rear wheel to the '56.

With the axle already centered and the wheel installed, you usually have 1 inch on either side of the swing arm.

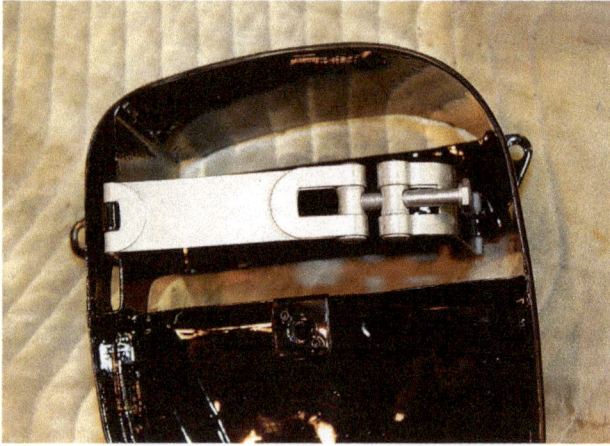

The accessory box with battery strap installed.

Now the accessory box has been mounted to the rear frame section. Note: some of the wiring work is already started.

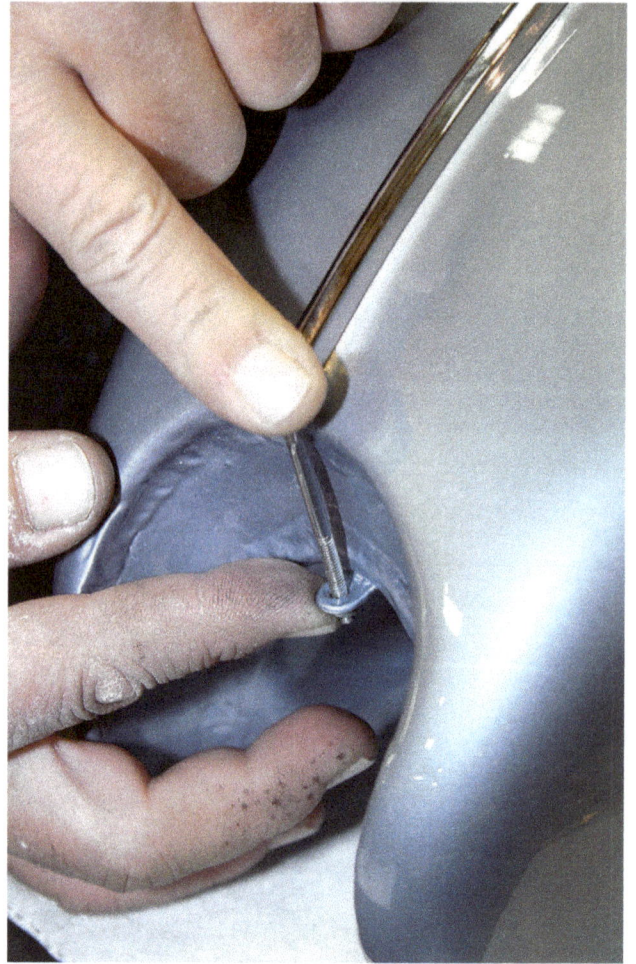

I push down on the styling strip at back of tank to install the small nut. Note: always start at the front and work to the back.

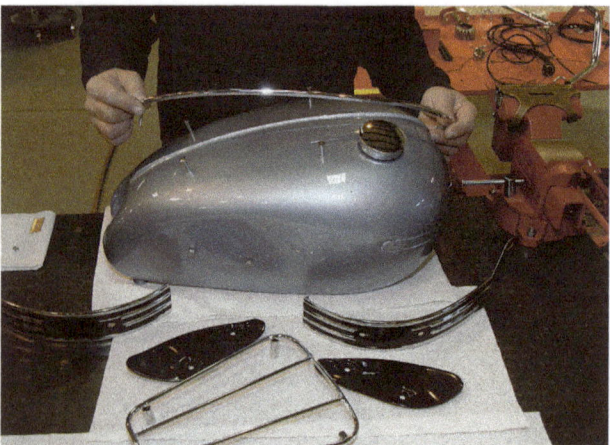

Gas tanks on the pre-unit bikes are made up of a lot of pieces, here I'm installing the center styling strip.

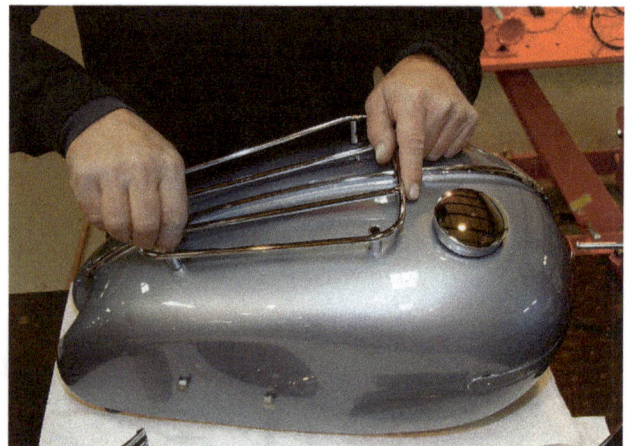

With the styling strip in place, installation of the parcel grid is next.

After bolting on the trim and the metal base, we can put on the knee pad rubber.

The oil tank and related components.

Time now to bolt the gas tank to the frame.

Danny and I install the '56 oil tank into the frame.

Detail shot of the gas tank bottom, note the rubber grommet and 5/16 inch shoulder bolt.

The gas tank, oil tank and accessory box completed.

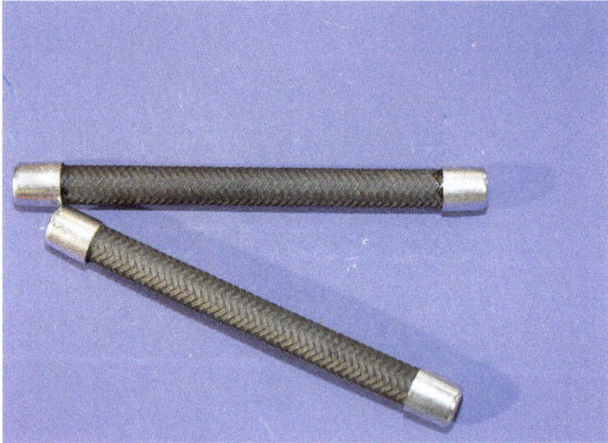

These are the correct, 5/16 inch, herringbone oil lines.

Here are the oil lines installed to the oil tank and feed pipe.

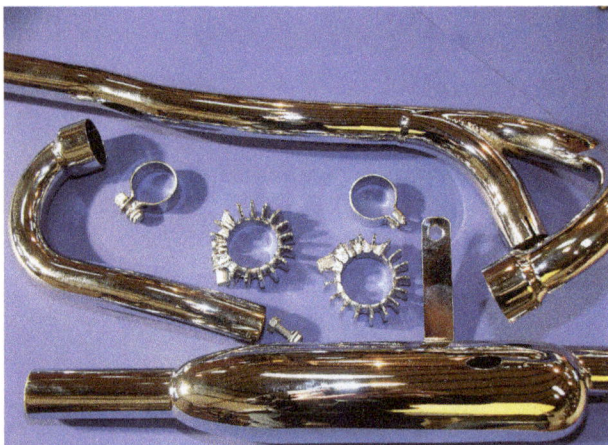

We start the exhaust work by putting on the right side pipe.

The complete layout of the TR6C exhaust.

Installation of the left side exhaust pipe is next.

1. Finally it's time to put the muffler on our TR6C.

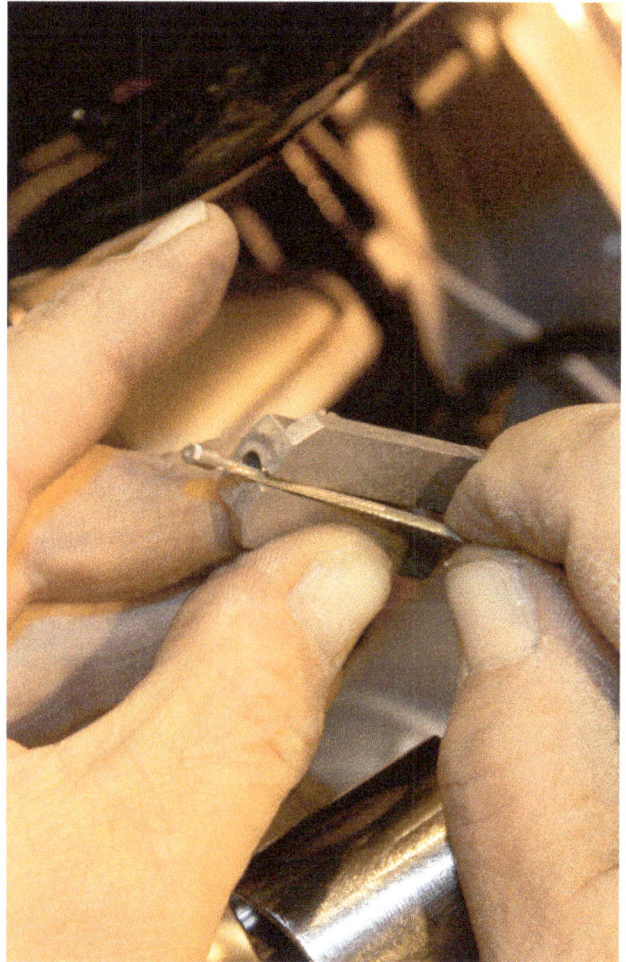

2. The carburetor and throttle assembly complete with cable before installation on the bike.

3. Installing choke cable through the choke slide.

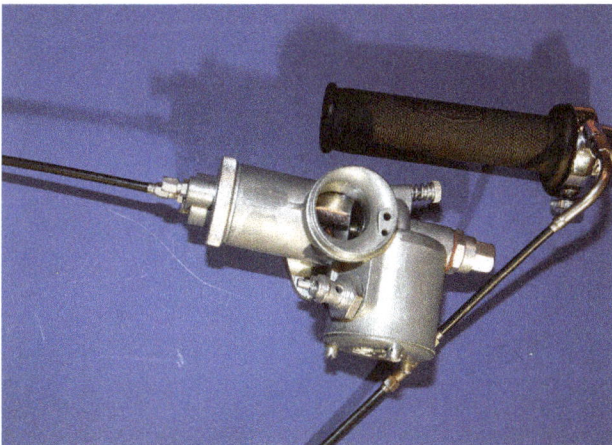

4. The slide and choke assembly prior to installation in the carburetor

5. With choke slide and throttle valve assembly complete, install both into the carburetor..

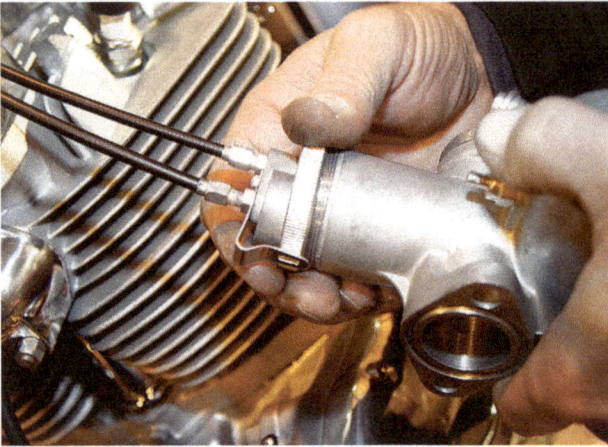

... now tighten the cap on the carburetor.

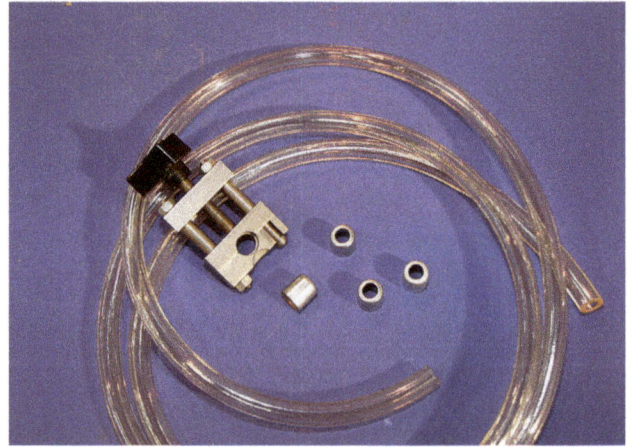

This is the correct clear gas line and gas line cups, with the crimping tool we use.

Here's the complete carburetor mounted to the engine, note the gas lime routing.

This crimping tool is easy to use...

... and does a nice neat crimp. These crimpers are readily available.

Day 5. After five, 12 hour days the 1956 TR6C is 95% complete.

Finally outside, and 100% complete.

Wiring

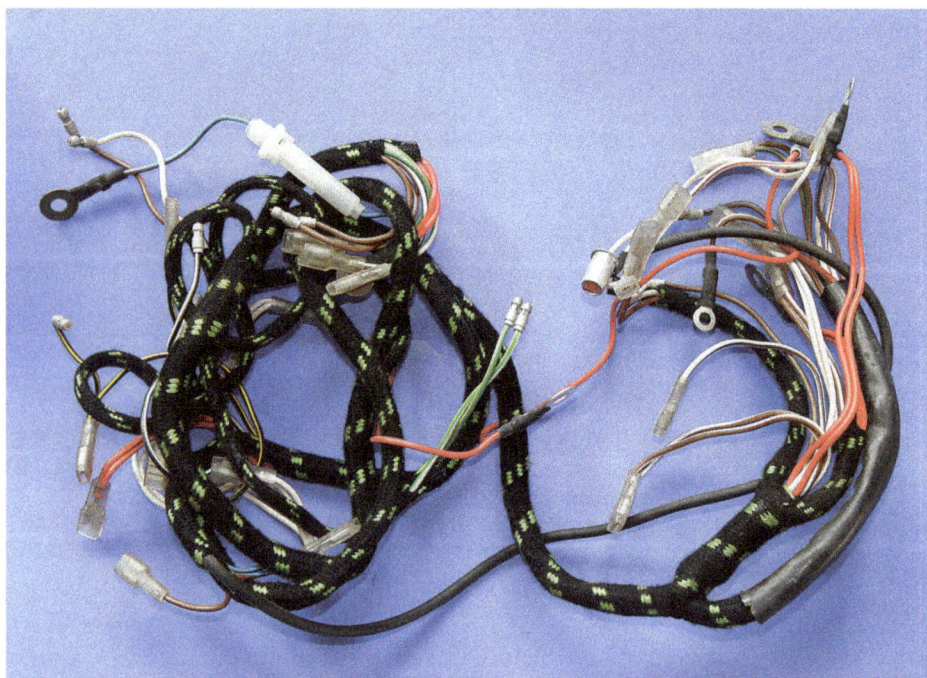

Compared to a modern motorcycle, the harness for a Triumph is pretty simple. Installation requires that you follow the schematic, and exhibit good attention to detail.

When it comes to restoring a triumph, you have to decide what to do about the wiring.

Unless the original harness is in good condition, you're going to need a complete new harness. Sometimes you can find a nice original harness, maybe at a swap meet, for example. There are also some good aftermarket harnesses available from the typical suppliers mentioned throughout the book.

Like other parts of restoring an old bike, neatness counts here. Any photos you took of the bike before disassembly will help with determining some of the details, like the exact routing of a wire or subharness. If you ask Garry how hard the wiring really is, he reports that it's not that tough. "In terms of whether of not someone working at home can install a new wiring harness, I think it's pretty simple. The whole thing is color-coded, it's pretty straightforward. I like to have a book near by with the schematic - there are several good books that include the wiring diagram. Basically, all you have to do is follow the diagram. Anybody with a little common mechanical knowledge can wire up one of these bikes.

Here you can see the wiring has been started in the headlight bucket.

Brake light switch and hardware...

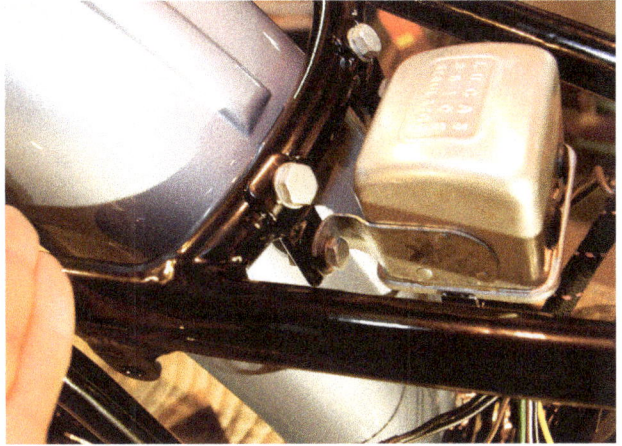

A regulator unit type RB107 is installed to the rear section frame.

... which mounts to the rear passenger foot peg bracket.

Note the way the tail light leads come through the hole in the rear fender.

Installing the wiring harness to the regulator

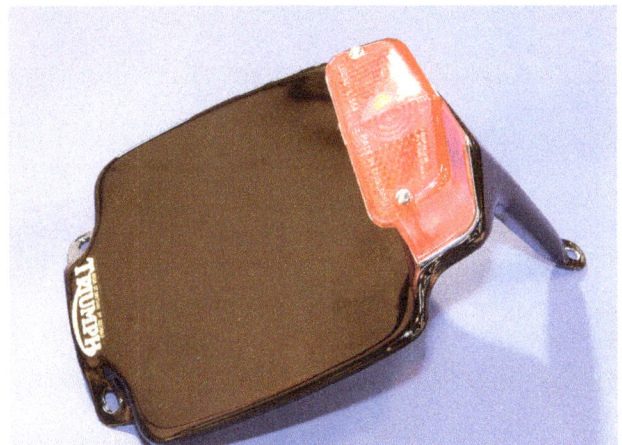

The rear tail light assembly complete.

Paint

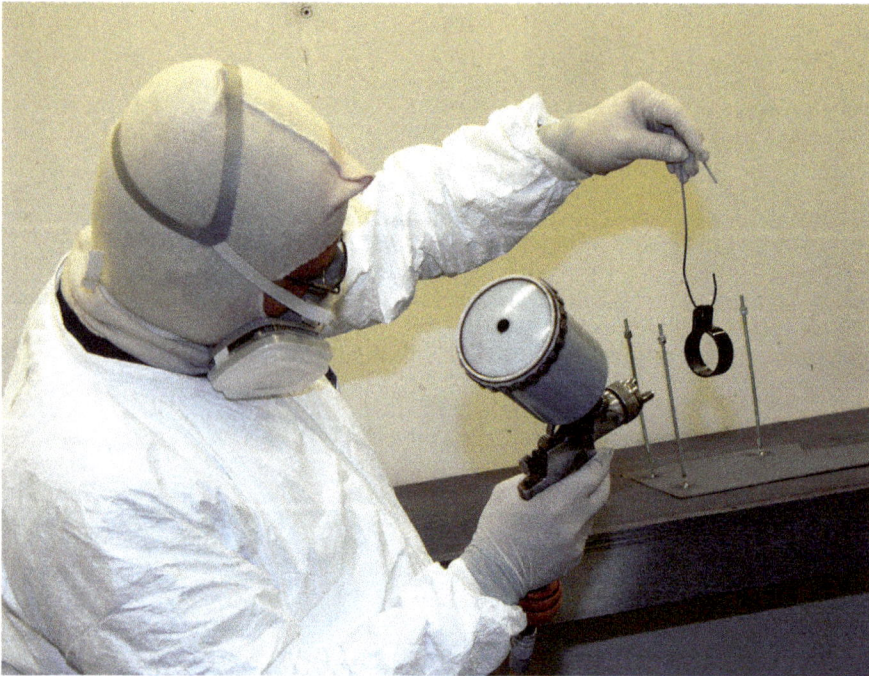

Here I'm in the paint booth spraying single stage gloss black on the front fork tube fender bracket. The paint I use is Dupont ChromaBase, either black or shell blue sheen. All of it comes from Don Hutchinson.

Some of the black TR6C parts hanging to dry in the booth.

When it comes to paint, Garry Chitwood is definitely old school. "When I can, I still use lacquer paint, but the problem these days is, there's very little of it left out there, it's going away. So the next choice is a urethane basecoat-clearcoat. The urethanes are pretty good, and the color match is perfect. Whether it's lacquer or urethane, we always get our paint from Don Hudson in Massachusetts."

If Garry has a secret for his flawless paint jobs, it's flawless preparation. "We take a lot of time and effort with each paint job. First, we make sure that the booth is clean and dust free, clean the floor, then we start shooting."

"After we have all the metal done, we put primer down. You have to make sure to go back and sand that primer to get it all smoothed out. Take the time to eliminate any dimples or dents that were missed earlier. Long before you put it in paint, be sure all the prep work is done and that the parts in the booth are clean."

"The gun I use is an HVLP gun from SATA. It's a nice gun and works well for me, but they are expensive. For a person at home though, you can get a nice gun for a hundred dollars, or a little more. That makes more sense for someone who might only use the gun a few times each year."

"The mistake most first time painters make is they skimp on the preparation, and the prep work is the key to doing a good paint job."

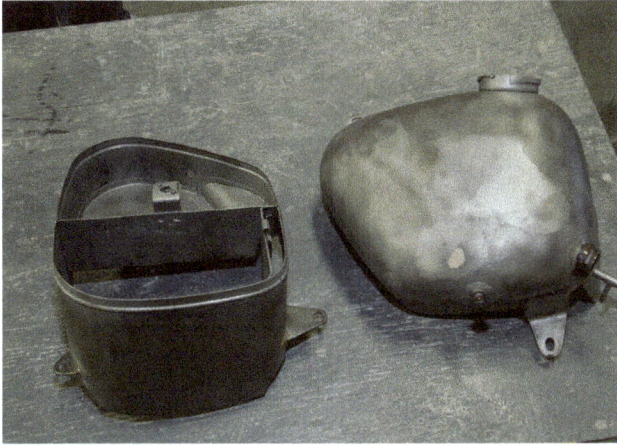

We like to strip all the old paint off the sheet metal parts in the bead-blast cabinet. Check for cracks and broken mounting tabs.

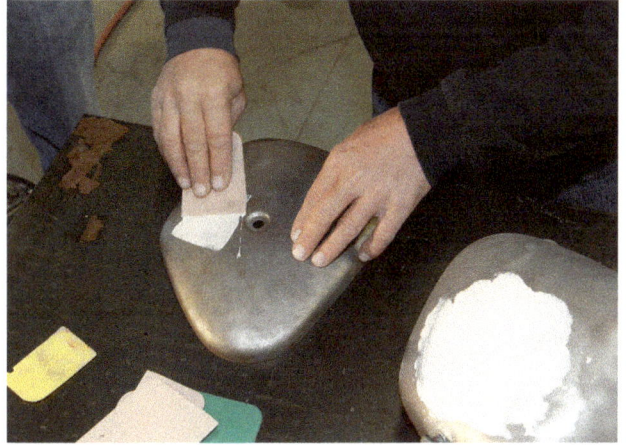

The outside accessory box cover gets the same treatment, a thin coat of spot putty.

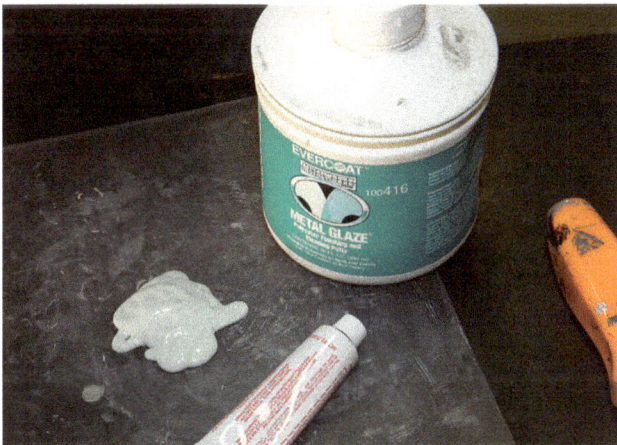

I like to use two-part spot putty, it's good for filling small dents and imperfections.

The spot putty dries fast, so the process goes quickly.

Mix the putty thoroughly, and spread it like frosting on a cake. I like to use thin coats of the putty. You can always do a second coat if needed.

Once the putty has dried, we begin the sanding with 180 grit paper, and finish with 320 before applying the first coat of primer.

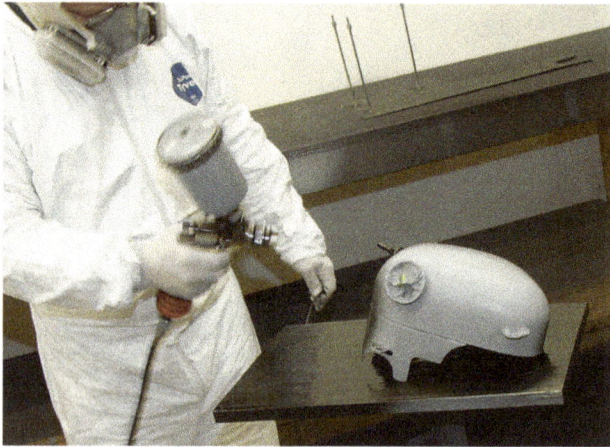

After priming the tank with primer I start with the first coat of single stage gloss black urethane.

Here I'm starting the application of the clearcoats. I like to put on 6 to 8 coats of clear, so I can sand and buff without worrying that I might sand through.

Next, I like to apply a total of 3 to 4 more wet coats of the single stage black.

We let the black dry for the recommended period of time before applying the clearcoat. The parts look great now, but wait until they're cleared and buffed.

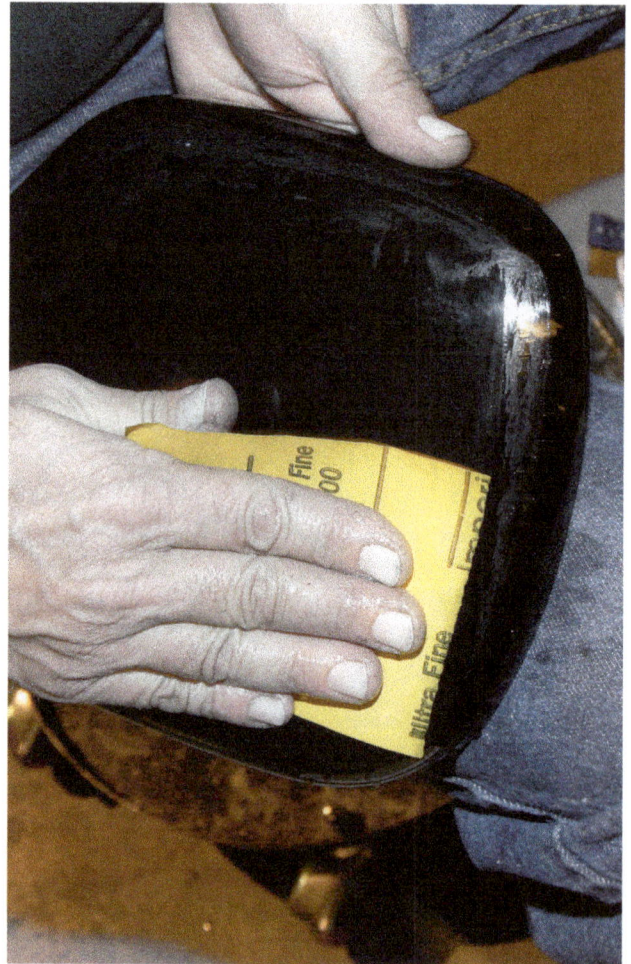

Once the clear is dry, I start the sanding with 2000 grit paper wet...

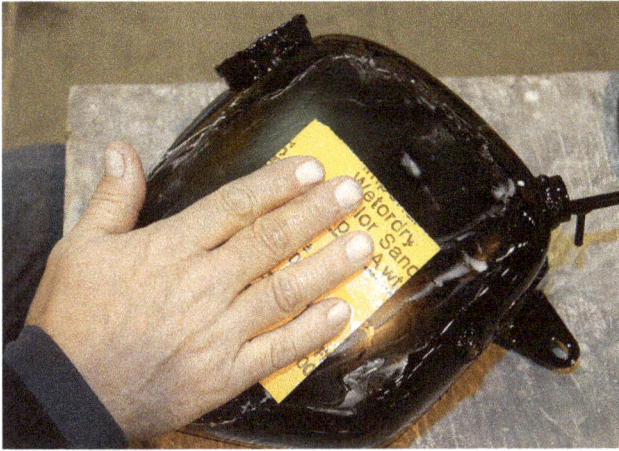

1. ...unless there's trash in the paint, then I might start with 1000 or 1500 grit paper.

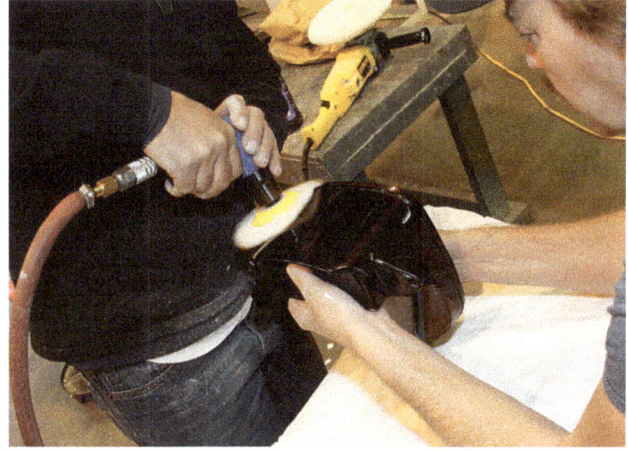

5. An extra set of hands is good, as the parts are small and there's no good way to clamp them in place.

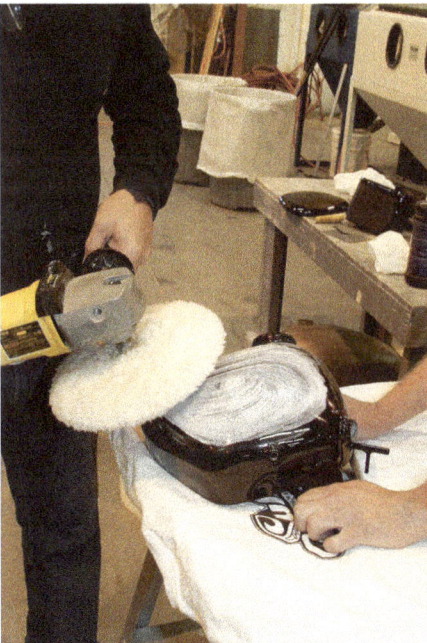

2. In this case, after sanding with 1500, we use a buffer and rubbing compound on the oil tank.

3. I like this rubbing compound from 3M.

4. For some of the smaller items I use the smaller air-powered buffer.

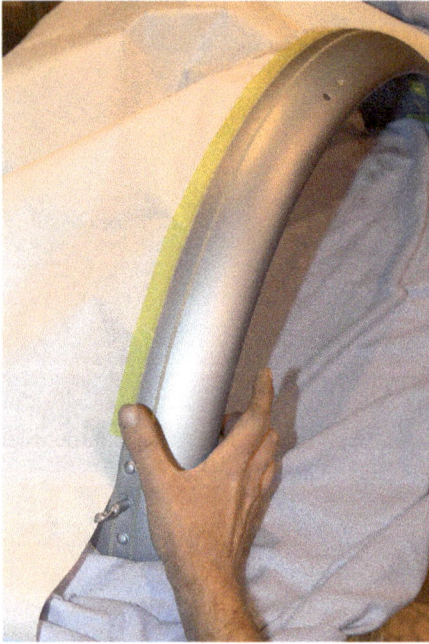

For the fenders we start by spraying two coats of Silver. Once that is dry I mask off the stripe in two steps, starting with the fineline tape and finishing with masking paper.

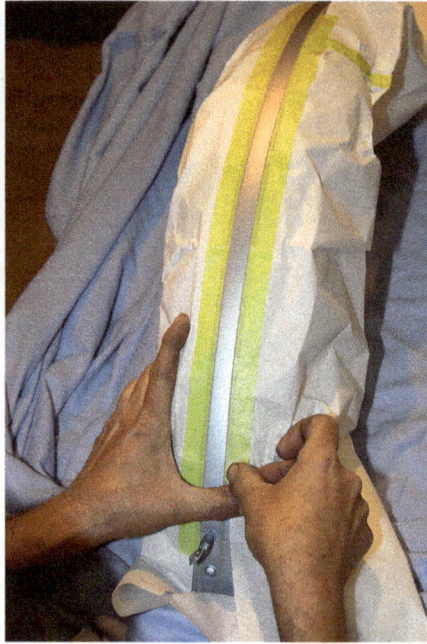

At this point Danny is almost finished taping off the fender's center stripe. He puts the edge of the wider masking tape on the center of the fineline tape.

I'm using single stage black paint again to paint in the center stripe.

After the center strip is painted and dries, I tape off the pinstripe using 1/8 inch tape.

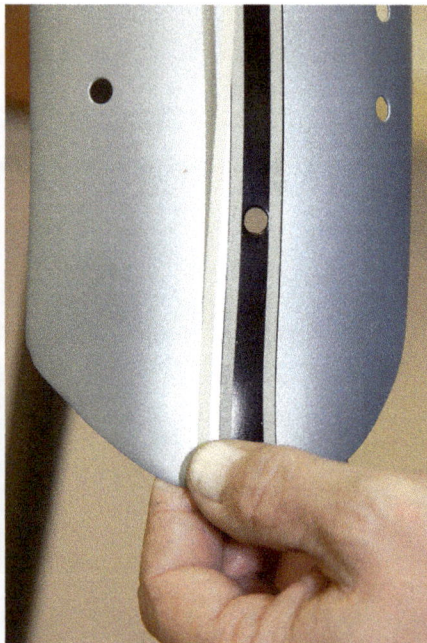

Using the 1/8 inch tape, I've created about a 3/16 inch gap for the pinstripe.

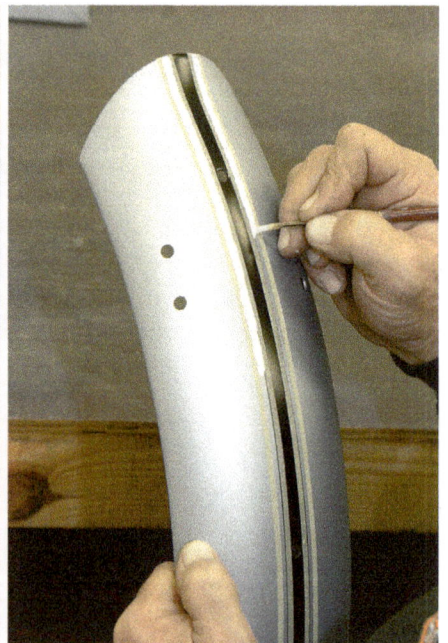

Once the taping is finished I use a small brush and white enamel paint to create the pinstripe.

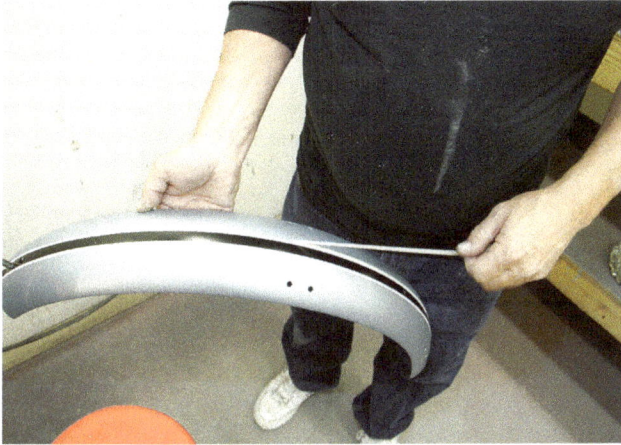

1. After the white pinstripe has been brushed in, remove the 1/8 inch pinstripe tape to reveal...

2. ...a nice, uniform straight-edged pinstripe.

4. The front and rear fenders after the clearcoats - we applied a total of 7 coats of paint to each fender.

3. The pinstripe has dried, I put down the clearcoats on both fenders.

Chapter Four

How to Buy an old Triumph

Advice from Randy Baxter

For most people, Marne, Iowa is the kind of sleepy little village that the state is famous for. Vintage motorcycle enthusiasts know better. They know that this small town located between Des Moines and Omaha is home to Baxter Cycle, the mother lode for anyone with an interest in old English motorcycles. And although Randy Baxter and his staff service and sell all the vintage English bikes, Triumphs seem to be the marque closest to Randy's heart. Which makes him the go-to guy for anyone looking for some advice prior to purchasing an old Trumpet, in this case, a pre-unit model.

You never know where you're going to find an old Triumph. Good, original bikes, are hard to find and tend to go for a premium. If there's any question about the bike's condition, or the originality of the parts, it's a good idea to bring along a bona fide expert to ensure you don't make an expensive mistake.

Randy, can we start by talking about the pre-unit bikes in a general sense, before we get down to the nuts and bolts of buying one of these bikes?

These bikes don't stand up to abuse as well as a unit Triumph. A good example is the primary chain. On a pre-unit bike the primary chain is smaller than the rear drive chain, so if you abuse the bike the primary chain breaks which busts up the primary case. That primary chain has only about 60% of the strength of the rear chain.

You have to remember that these bikes were treated differently here in the US that they were overseas. In England, especially back in the post war period, you had a car or a bike, but not both. For working people, the bike was their only form of transportation. They didn't race it and they didn't beat the piss out of the bike. In the states you had a car first, then you bought the bike for fun. It was not your primary form of transportation. If you broke the bike you still had a car to drive. They were looked at differently and ridden differently.

Which pre-unit Triumph do I want to buy, in terms of the different years and models, how do I decide?

The newer they, are the better they are. Triumph discontinued babbit rod bearings in about 1955. Bikes built after that year are easier to rebuild, it's obviously a much better system. That was a big milestone. If you want to buy a pre-unit bike, keep in mind what it has for rod bearings.

Randy Baxter, of Baxter Cycle fame, has sold literally thousands of Triumphs. Today, he tends to have 40 to 50 vintage Triumphs in-house at any given time, along with a huge stock of parts.

Though it's not a 1959, this 1960 T120 owned by Bobby Sullivan is still a pre-unit early Bonneville, and thus very valuable.

The newer crank and rod assemblies use insert bearings, which makes the engines much easier to rebuild, as opposed to babbit bearings used in the earlier bikes.

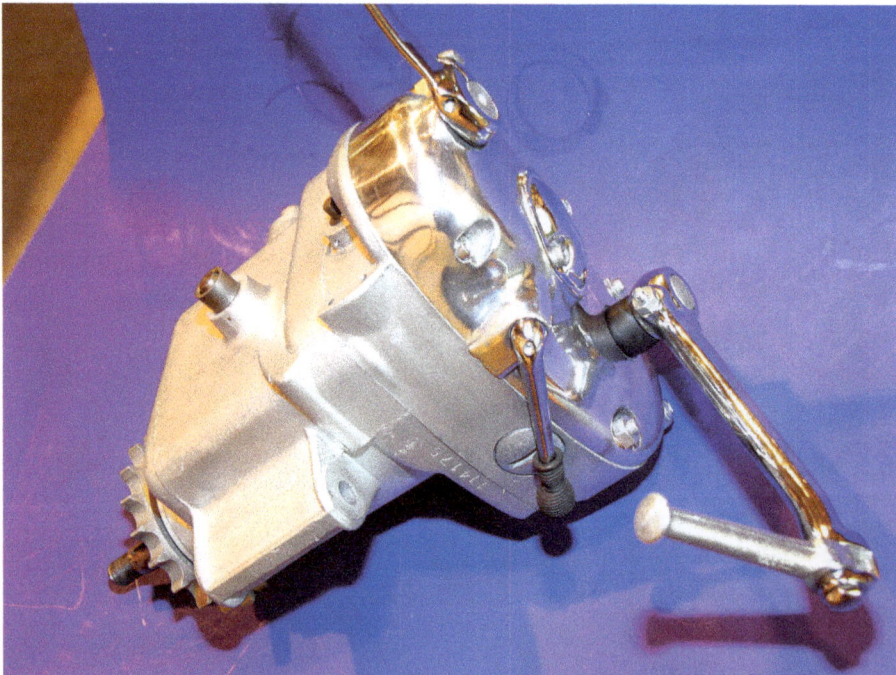

When buying a complete pre-unit bike, or a transmission for a pre-unit, be sure to check the transmission case for cracks at the mounting points. Be sure to check the case for evidence of welding or earlier repairs.

For anyone who has the old babbit bearings, we can take the old cranks and modify them to accept newer rods with insert bearings.

What are some of the things to watch for when I'm looking at potential bikes I might buy?

Always check the mating numbers on the case halves. The number is at the front or bottom of each case half. If the numbers match, then it hasn't been blown up so bad that someone had to replace a case.

Always check the transmission case, has it been welded? Are there stress cracks where the mounting bolts go through the case? The internals are pretty durable on those early four-speeds, it's essentially the same four-speed used in later unit bikes.

Another big problem is the alloy heads. There's often a crack between the valve seat and the stud hole. They always have at least one crack. It won't stop them from running. When you have the head apart, you have to grind and weld the crack. We often drill the stud hole out to the next size and press in a hollow dowel. The eight-stud heads are all alloy. Because most of them have been rebuilt so many times, the seats are generally beat to oblivion, that can be a tricky repair that's best done by a good shop.

Do you need an expert to help evaluate a bike prior to giving up your hard earned cash?

If you don't know the seller, then it is worth the money to bring someone along, rather than make a big mistake. The serial numbers are very important. From 1950 on, they should have matching engine and frame numbers. The model number is not on the frame. The "6T" for example is on the motor, but may not be on the frame. You can fix a lot of things, but you can't fix altered numbers. If the engine and frame numbers are mismatched, it's not the end of the world, engines did get swapped out, but it diminishes the value of the bike.

This is one area where it would be worth having someone who's an expert look at the bike to be sure the numbers match. These bikes are getting to be worth $20,000.00, so there's an incentive to re-stamp. Some altered numbers are so obvious Stevie Wonder could see the problem, but others are pretty good.

Are values going up faster for pre-unit, than for unit bikes?

They are both going up at about the same rate. Some pre-units are worth a lot more than others. The best are the 1959 to 1962 Bonnies. Some pre-unit TR6 and TR5s bring really good money. And the real competition bikes are worth a lot.

1938 to 1940 is the golden era for pre-unit Triumphs and the absolute golden era for British motorcycles. The bikes took a big evolutionary leap with the speed twins. It propelled motorcycling into the next big phase. It's like what Honda did with their 750cc four-cylinder bikes. Those early Speed Twins were great, with the girder fork and the big headlight.

What about buying a bike at an auction, are there things to watch out for, a separate set of guidelines for buyers?

The first thing is to allow yourself enough time. Go the day before and do the previews. Look really hard at the bikes. If there's a bike you

like, try to track down the owner and talk to him. Always get as much information about the bike as you can.

Or talk to the auction staff. Seek out someone at the auction who may be an expert. Take a look at the paper work. The title work might offer clues. An old title may mean it's been owned by the same guy for a long time.

You have to be careful to avoid an impulse buy. It's too easy to stick your hand up and suddenly realize, later, that you paid too much. Do your homework before and avoid impulse buying. Be sure to find out what the buyer's premium is.

The title is the fly in the ointment. After you buy the bike, is the title OK, will it transfer? People buy a bike and often can't get it transferred. Each state is a little different, California is one of the worst.

What about buying a bike on Ebay?

Ebay is one of the worst places to buy anything vintage mechanical. I have customers who buy off eBay if they can drive to the location and actually look at the bike. Sometimes I will go and look for them. At least contact the seller and ask all the right questions, and look for red flags.

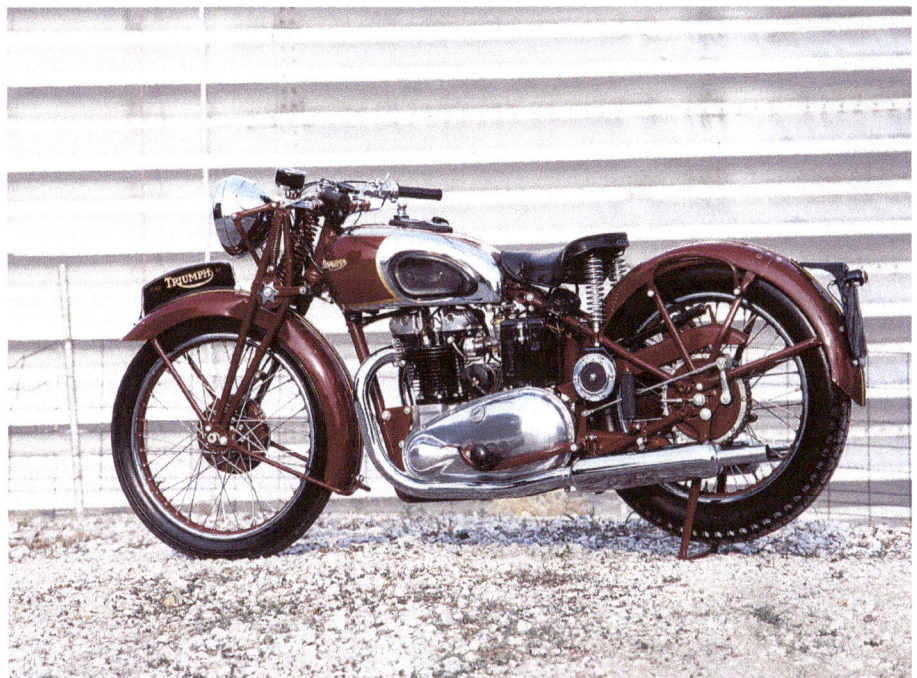

The Speed Twin changed the landscape for motorcycles. As such, the early examples like this 1940 model are very valuable.

The really old Triumphs hold a certain cachet, and a high value. Before buying one to restore however, beware; parts for bikes like this 1932, owned by Alan Berry, can be very hard to find.

Are the photos vague, is the copy vague, are they telling you things about Triumphs in general, but nothing about this particular bike? If possible go look at the bike or have someone else look at it.

If possible, also go and ride the bike. Look at the feedback on the guy, check his seller rating on eBay, that will tell you something.

I don't recommend eBay. In most cases you have no recourse. No matter what, it's yours. The guys that did well on eBay did all the things I said. They asked the right questions and got the right pictures.

There are so many horror stories about the electrics on the English bikes, how good or bad are the electrical components on these pre-unit bikes?

Before 1952, pre-Lucas, the bikes had a slightly better magneto. Magnetos work when they work, and are a real pain when they don't. If you buy a bike with a magneto, it's a good idea to take it off and send it out for a rebuild. That way you know what you have, and know that it will work correctly. When they get old they loose magnetism. Or the condenser goes bad, and the condenser is buried inside. Be sure to have the magnets recharged when you have the magneto serviced or rebuilt. The charging system is weak on these old bikes too. There are some solid-state regulators available that are a big improvement on the original regulators.

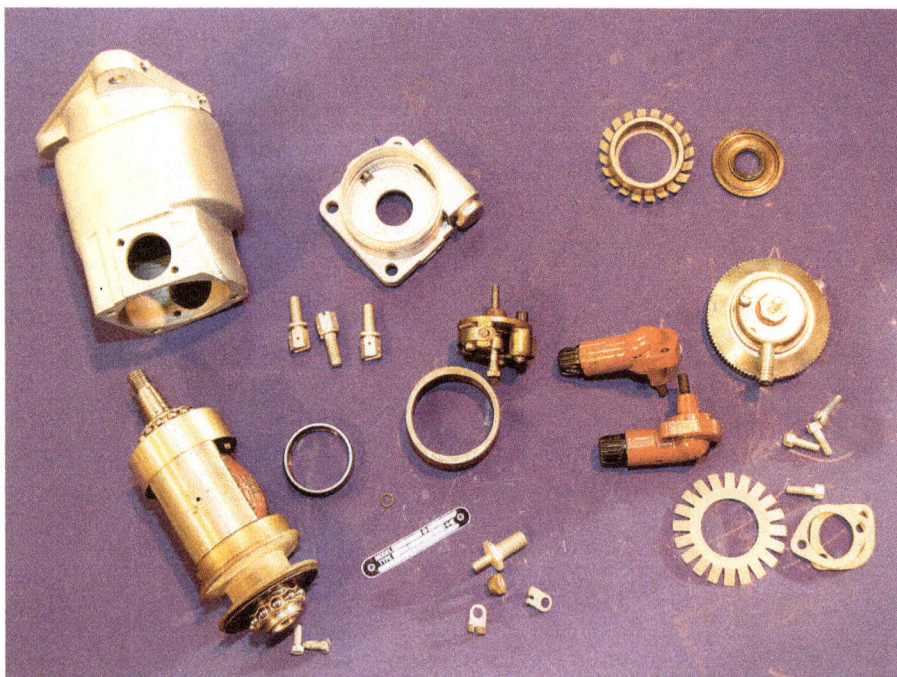

The magneto might be called the heart of your Triumph. If you intend to ride the bike, be sure to have the magneto overhauled by a good specialist during the restoration.

On some of the alternator bikes, the ones with the smaller stator, you can replace the stator with a more modern 12v stator, and convert the whole bike to 12 volts.

Is it hard to get parts for the pre-unit bikes?

Parts are not hard to get considering the age of these machines. A lot of stuff is available, we have a big inventory of pre-unit parts at our store. Parts availability is as good as it's ever been. The quality of most of those parts is also pretty good.

It is however, hard to find good used heads, though they do make all the internal parts. New cylinder barrels are available. There is some poor re-pop sheet metal, but also some stuff that's as good or better then NOS, it's more money of course. If you are doing a 100 point restoration, you want the English fenders from Ace Classics. Good gas tanks are harder to find, and the original tanks are often in rough condition.

What percentage of the bikes that you have in stock at Baxter Cycle are pre-unit, as compared to the Unit bikes?

Typically we will have from 6 to 12 pre-unit Triumphs, and 25 to 35 unit bikes, for sale at any time.

Any final words of wisdom, regarding the pre-unit Triumphs?

You have to understand that these bikes are more work to restore and repair than the later bikes. There are more parts on a pre-unit. A pre-unit gas tank, for example, is made up of fifty-some parts including the bolts and the trim.

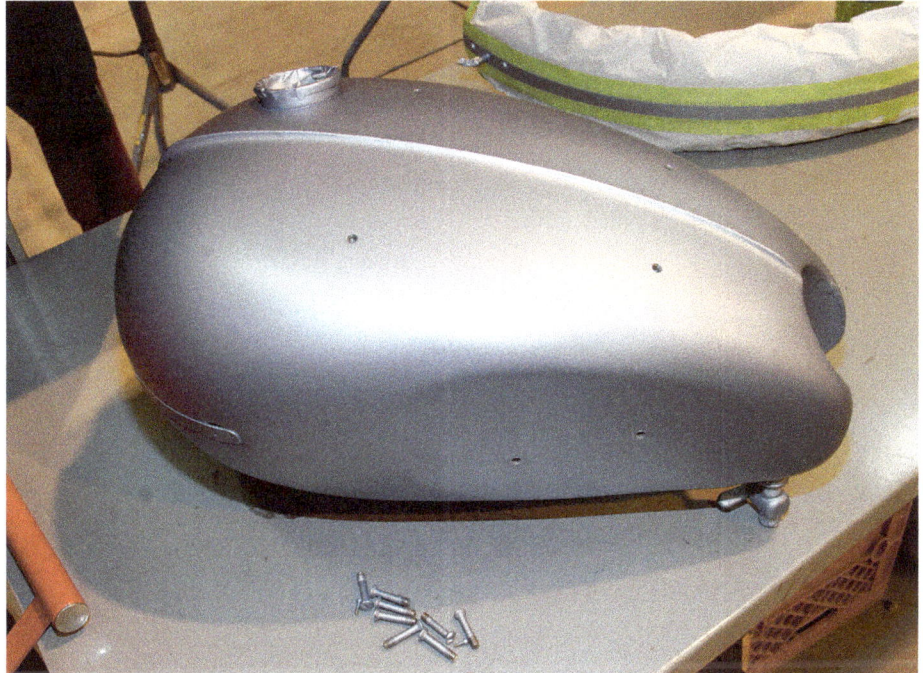

The tanks and fenders, tanks especially, tend to catch hell on an old bike. When buying, check that the tank is in good condition and not rusted out along the bottom. Good replacement sheet metal is hard to find and expensive when you do.

Most of the major parts are still available for bikes like these two Blackbirds belonging to Mike Crone. It's finding the little parts and the sheet metal that often proves challenging.

Chapter Five

Gallery

A Visual Guide

Service manuals and the more typical restoration guides are all good tools when you are tying to assemble an old Triumph into a bike that looks exactly as it did when new. On the other hand, there's noting like a good photograph to explain exactly how to route a cable or which chain guard to use on a certain model. Thus we give you a collection of what we think are "correct" pre-unit Triumphs. The one thing we can't swear to is the paint color of the photos. Because of all the variables in the photo and printing end of things, we can't guarantee the colors match the originals.

The pre-unit of pre-units, the '59 Bonneville. These two beauties are the handiwork of Baxter Cycle.

When Triumph introduced the Thunderbird they bumped the displacement from 500 to 650cc, all in an effort to please the young men on the other side of the pond, and stay ahead of the the other English bike manufacturers.

Another Mike Crone bike, this 1951 T-bird looks ready to run.

Because the Speed Twin was introduced before the war, we often forget that Triumph continued to manufacture the bike well up into the 1950s.

Property of Mike Crone, this particular Speed Twin is from 1955. Note the swoopy front fender and the hydraulic suspension used on both ends.

The T110 was the road burner of its day, and the first Triumph model to come with true rear suspension. The new suspended frame meant a complete redesign of the bike.

Property of Mike Crone, this '56 T110 uses the big-for-the-day 8 inch front brake drum. With a single Amal monobloc carb and 8.5 to 1 compression, the T110 was rated at 42 horses. 1956 was the first year for the aluminum cylinder head.

Seen elsewhere in the book, this Chitwood restored '56 TR6 uses a 650cc engine that inhaled through a single Amal Monobloc, and exhaled into a two-into-one system that runs along the bike's left side.

1956 was the first year for the legendary TR6. The bike was created in typical Triumph fashion, by placing a 650cc engine in a 500cc bike. Viola, instant hot rod.

Like the first-year TR6, this 1957 model uses the two-into-one exhaust. This '57 model uses a magneto for spark and a generator to keep the lights shining bright (so to speak).

The TR6 uses the 8 inch front drum brake seen first on the T110. As a competition bike the TR6 used only slim fenders on both ends, unlike the valanced and "tubed" fenders seen on many other Triumphs from the same period.

This Bonneville from 1960 shows how the bike evolved from a twin-carb T110 to a twin-carb TR6 with street tires. Larger bulge in the primary cover means this bike is alternator-equipped.

Owned by Greg Hult, this 1960 Bonneville uses two gauges mounted in their own housing, just above the stand-alone chrome plated headlight housing.

Because the TR6 started life as an off road machine, it came without the valanced fenders and headlight nacelle.

This 1960 TR6 owned by Baxter Cycle carries the correct aztec red and ivory paint.

1962 might be called the year that Triumph took a deep breath, before introducing the new unit bikes in 1963. Thus, this Bonneville is the last to use the duplex frame and separate engine and transmission.

Though the Bonnevilles and TR6s from the late 1960s are all the rage, it's hard to fault the grace and poise of this Greg-Hult-owned pre-unit Bonnie.

I bought this 1962 TR6SS from the original owner in California. The bike was pretty rough, it had the wrong front fender and a bobbed rear fender. The letters SS stand for Super Sport, these bikes came in from Canada, some kind of dealer swap between US and Canadian dealers.

This bike came with a speedo and no tachometer. 1962 was the last year for the duplex frame, but this one must have been a late-'62 model, because the frame is beefier at the neck, and some of the switches are the same as the switches used on the '63 and '64 bikes.

Chapter Six

Keep 'em Running

Motorcycles, not Sculpture

In the wilds of southeastern Minnesota, amid farms and fields, lies a small business essential to many a die-hard British bike fan. From the road all you see is a concrete driveway and a small group of buildings. And though the place is very neat and the buildings all look new, it's what's inside the buildings that counts. Klempf's British Parts is the result of over thirty years of hard work by Mitch Klempf. What started as a part time job, turned into a more-than-full-time operation that consumes three buildings and requires the attention of Mitch, his wife, and one employee.

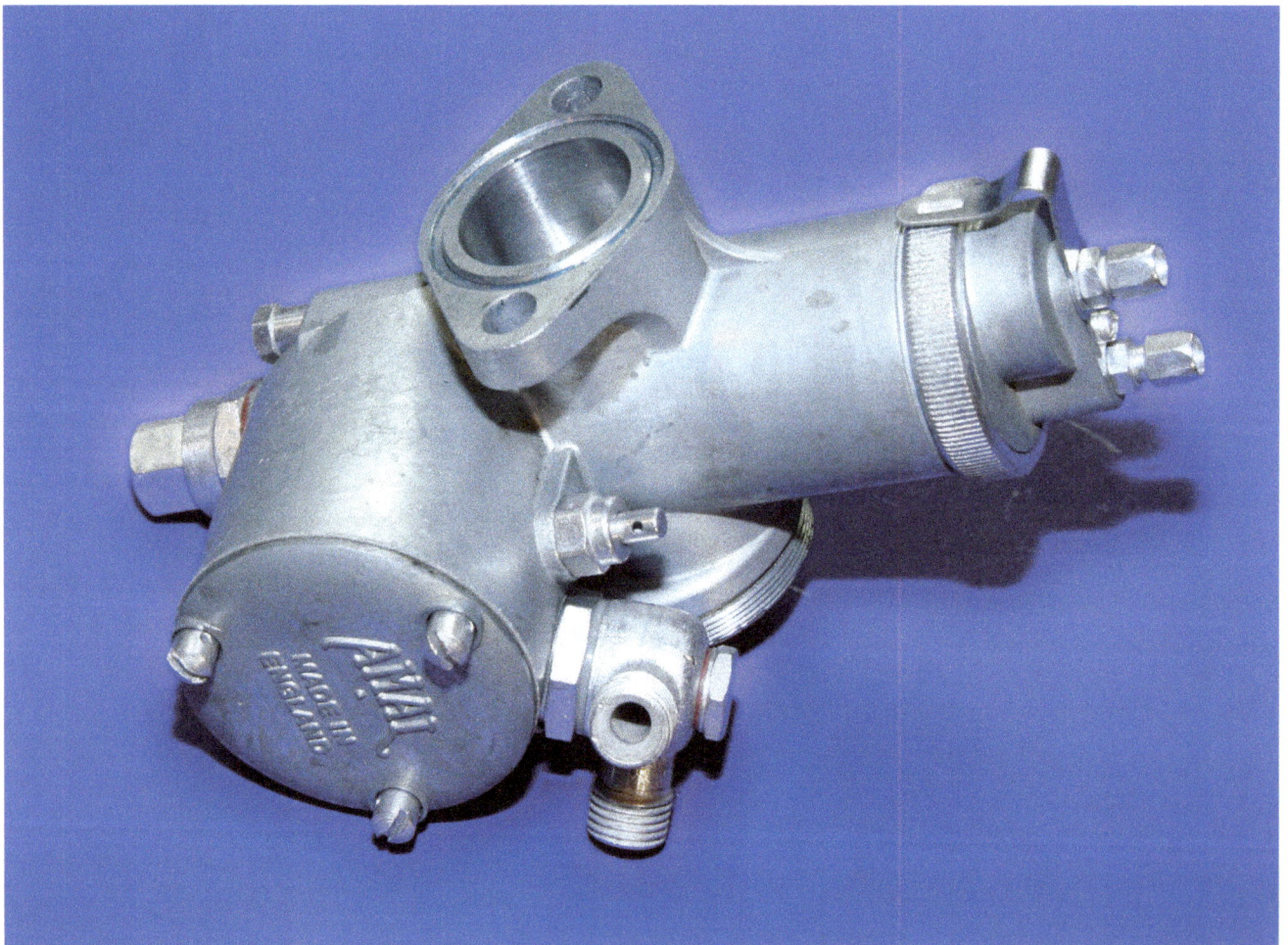

Mitch has parts for the often maligned Monobloc carbs by Amal - they're really not quite as bad as everyone says. Or you can convert to a later model Concentric model carburetor.

The subject of this book is old motorcycles, bikes that are at best nearly fifty years old. Too many of these bikes spend their days in the corner of the garage or shop, talking in whispers with other old bikes. Reminiscing about the good old days of high speed runs down two lane roads, the loving maintenance performed by a caring owner, and the anticipation of the next run.

In order to keep more of those old British bikes running we've come to Klempf's to ask Mitch just what it takes to use one of these bikes on a regular basis. To ensure they don't spend their days tucked into a dusty corner. To convince riders that these are indeed motorcycles, meant to be ridden, repaired, and ridden again.

Q&A, MITCH KLEMPF

Mitch, can you start by telling us a little bit about how you became involved in motorcycles, and how you started the business?

I started riding motorcycles as a young kid. I had a Honda 90, but then I wanted something bigger so I bought a 1964 Bonneville. Most of the time, when the dealer fixed something, the bike would quit on the way home. And they didn't stock many parts, so you always had to wait two or three weeks for replacement parts. Two weeks during a short Minnesota summer is a long time. So I started to buy extra parts for my bike, and for working on other people's bikes.

The business grew out of those parts. People started to come to me for parts because they knew I had extras. It just grew from there. It started out as a part-time operation, now I work 12 or 14 hours most days, except Sundays.

Did you see the business getting this big?

No, not at the time. I just thought that as long as the business grew I would keep on working. The US was the biggest market for the Meriden Triumphs, so I knew there was potential. We work hard to earn our customer's business.

Sometimes when I go to get my car fixed, I wish they would give me the same respect that we give our motorcycle customers. Even now, with the bad economy, we are just as busy as ever, we must be doing something right.

Mitch Klempf started the business almost by accident, and now presides over a vast stock of parts for vintage English motorcycles.

The guy who answers the phone is usually Mitch. After more than thirty years in business, he not only knows the parts, he also knows which aftermarket parts are the best for your particular situation.

Do you sell just Triumph parts?

No, we have Triumph, BSA and Norton, from the mid 1950s up to 1982, to the end of Meriden bikes. We do have a few parts for earlier Brit bikes, but that's it, we don't do any of the Hinckley bikes.

Mostly we buy parts from other vendors, but sometimes we have parts manufactured. The Triumph Hurricane decals, for example, we had those manufactured and they just came in. We have over 18,000 line items.

What about the older pre-unit bikes, can these be used on a regular, or semi-regular basis?

Yes, but they are old. They suffer from metal fatigue. They were not made as heavy duty as the newer bikes. In many cases they're just worn out. These are not modern bikes, you can't just ride the wheels off them. You can't run 90 miles per hour with the modern bikes, and you do have to perform your maintenance.

Can you list some of the systems that can be converted to more modern components, in an effort to make them more reliable?

In some cases you can convert them to 12 volts. That way you can run better lights. The later alternator bikes can be converted to 12 volts.

The 1960, '61 and '62, bikes have the stator ring in the primary. With those you could use the later Lucas, high output, 12 volt

A variety of complete wiring harnesses are available for most of the pre-unit bikes, including an original Lucas harness assembly.

alternator. Some of the older bikes used the really big stator, and it's hard to convert those to a more modern alternator and a 12 volt system.

For generator bikes, there is a 12 volt conversion available, but they are expensive. Most of our customers don't want to spend that much money on that type of conversion.

Lucas used to make a 12 volt, electronic ignition that replaced the the whole magneto. That was a good ignition, but now they don't make it anymore. In some cases there isn't enough demand for anyone to manufacture the special parts, especially for pre-unit bikes.

With carburetors, the best thing that riders can do is keep them clean. You can't let the gas go stale and you can't let the gas evaporate in the float bowls. If there's any water in that gas, it will leave a white chalky residue behind that plugs up the circuits. You have to drain the carbs if the bike is going to sit for a month or more.

Some owners convert their bikes to the later Amal concentric carbs, they are more economical than the old carbs; and parts are more readily available, and reasonably priced.

If I own a pre-unit bike from the mid 1950s on up, can I still buy most of the parts I need to maintain and repair that bike?

Yes, most parts are still available, but for pre-unit bikes those parts are manufactured in smaller batches, so they might be more expensive than the same part for a unit bike. Some of the new parts are better than others. The sheet metal, for example. A lot of the re-pop stuff isn't really right. Some of the gas tanks just

aren't correct in their dimensions and shape. I don't know why anyone would go to the trouble of producing the tooling to manufacture a tank and not do it right, but they do. The headlight nacelle parts are hard to find too, especially ones that are manufactured correctly. If you buy a bike, try to buy one with all the correct body parts already on the bike.

The motor, transmission and clutch parts are all fairly available. A lot of those parts will remain on the market as long as there is demand, as long as people use the bikes and buy enough parts. When no one uses the stuff they will stop manufacturing those parts.

What are some of the other issues that come up when people try to repair and restore these bikes?

Paint is a problem because there are no paint codes. Some guys take the parts to a paint jobber with a scanner, and they supposedly can scan the color and mix up a perfect match. I send people to known Triumph painters, people like Don Hutchinson and Jason Small, they do paint that is considered correct and wins at the shows.

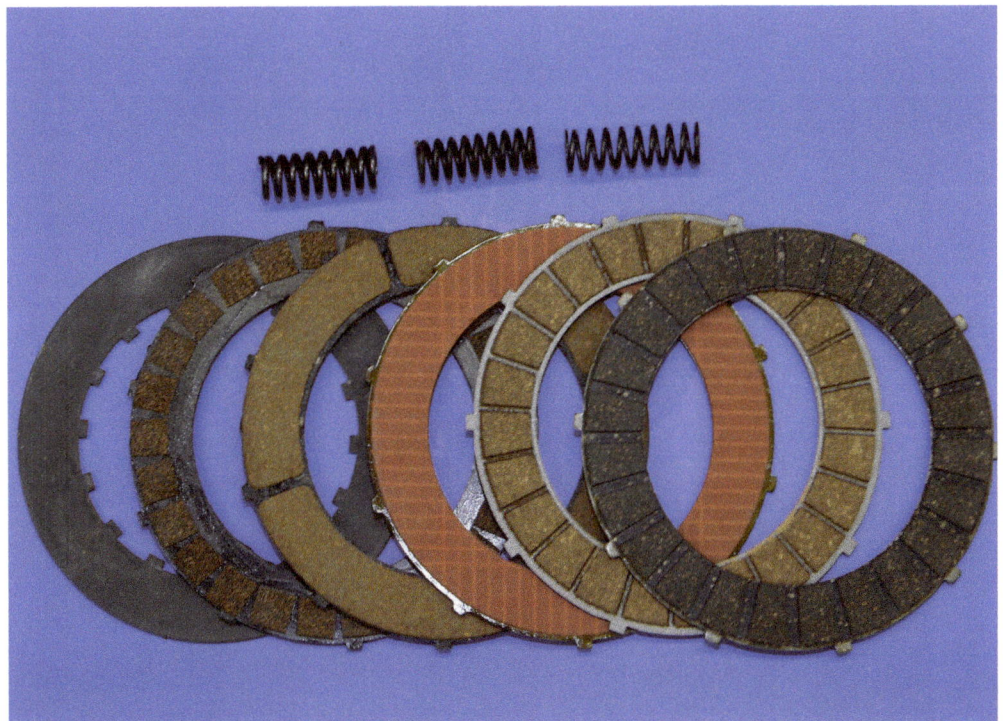

Like the wiring harnesses, clutch plates of different materials, and different quality levels, are available. Ask someone like Mitch which one is the best for you.

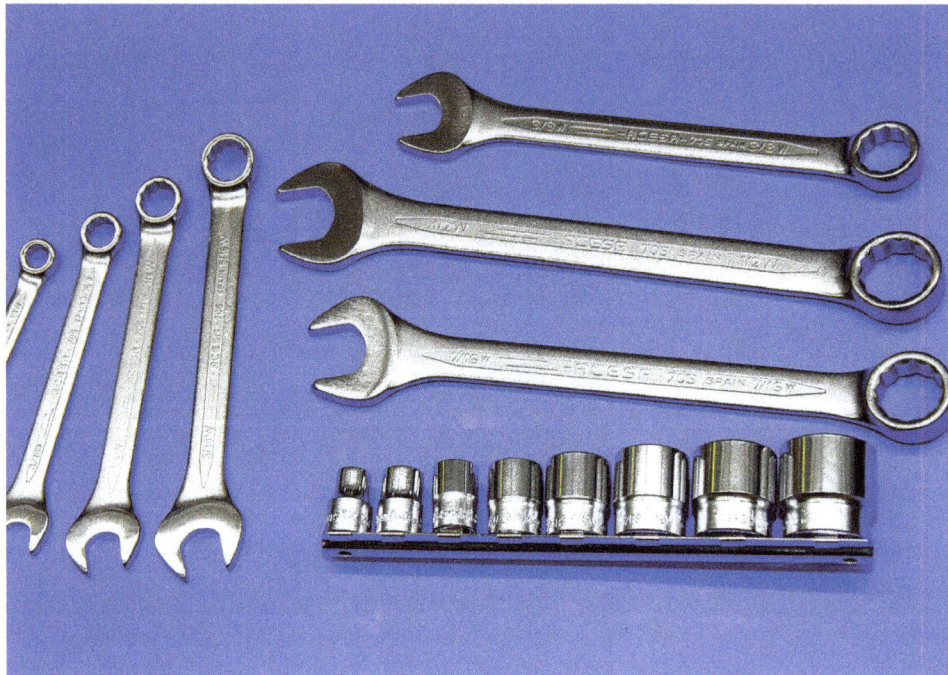

You can't always find an American (or SAE) size wrench that will fit a CEI or Whitworth head. These sets are available from Mitch, or any quality tool outlet.

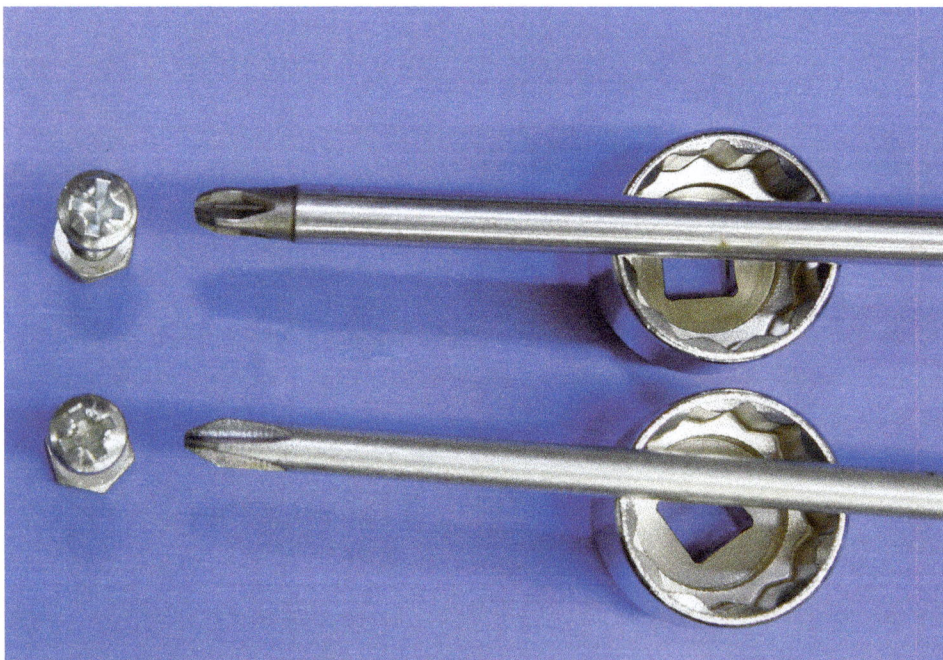

What looks like a typical Phillips-head fastener, top, is actually a British variant. Note the difference between the top screwdriver, called a posi-drive, and a standard Phillips screwdriver, bottom. Posi-drive can be found at Sears or the Snap-on truck. Use the right bit or you risk stripping the head of your screws.

What about wiring, people always complain about the Lucas parts?

The Lucas parts aren't really bad, they kind of got a bad rap. But remember, these bikes vibrate, so that is hard on the wiring and all the components. The Japanese wiring and components of the same period weren't any better, but those bikes didn't vibrate as much.

Are there other issues to watch out for?

The clutch can be a problem. Because the bikes sit too much, the clutch can seize up. So then guys will get them started and run them up against a wall, with the clutch lever pulled in, to break the clutch loose. A lot of times, what happens, the transmission explodes. If the clutch seizes, you have to take it apart, clean up the plates and put it back together. You may not even need new parts. If you try to break it apart it can be a two-thousand dollar mistake.

How about fasteners, people always have questions about the nuts and bolts?

People think these are all Whitworth bolts, but it's more complicated than that. Many of the bolts used on pre-unit Triumphs are CEI, or Cycle Engineers Institute (this system was later replaced by the BSC or British Standard Cycle).

There are actually two Whitworth thread systems (note the nearby chart), coarse and fine. The Whitworth threads use a 55 degree angle between threads, while the CEI threads use a 60 degree angle. So even when the diameter and the number of threads per inch are the same, you can not interchange a Whitworth for a CEI bolt. People use the wrong stuff all the time, they strip threads and cobble the things together.

People also don't know about posi-driv screwdrivers. These look like a typical Phillips head, but they are different. If you use a typical Phillips head screwdriver on the case screws you will strip out the head. We have socket sets and combination wrenches, and you can buy the Posi-driv screwdrivers from Snap-on or Sears.

Any Final Words of Advice?

Run good gas, do good maintenance. Riding is good for them and sitting isn't. Sometimes if they sit for a long time the oil will wet sump – the oil from the oil tank ends up in the bottom of the engine's crankcase. So if you check the oil before a ride and it's two quarts low, ask yourself, 'where did that oil go?', before you dump in two more quarts of oil. I tell people to check the oil when they come in from a ride, instead of when they leave on the next ride.

Threads Per Inch

Size	Cycle Engineers Institute (C.E.I.)	UNIFIED Unified Fine (UNF)	Unified Coarse (UNC)	WHITWORTH British Standard Fine (BSF)	British Standard Whitworth (Coarse) (BSW)
1/4"	26	28	20	26	20
5/16"	26	24	18	22	18
3/8"	26	24	16	20	16
7/16"	26	20	14	18	14
1/2"	20	20	13	16	12
9/16"	20	18	12	16	12
5/8"	20	18	11	14	11

Left to right, the differences between CEI, Unified (what we often call SAE) and Whitworth fasteners. Many of the fasteners on a pre-unit Triumph are CEI, not Whitworth. And even if the diameter and threads-per-inch are the same, that doesn't mean you can swap one fastener for the other, note the illustration below.

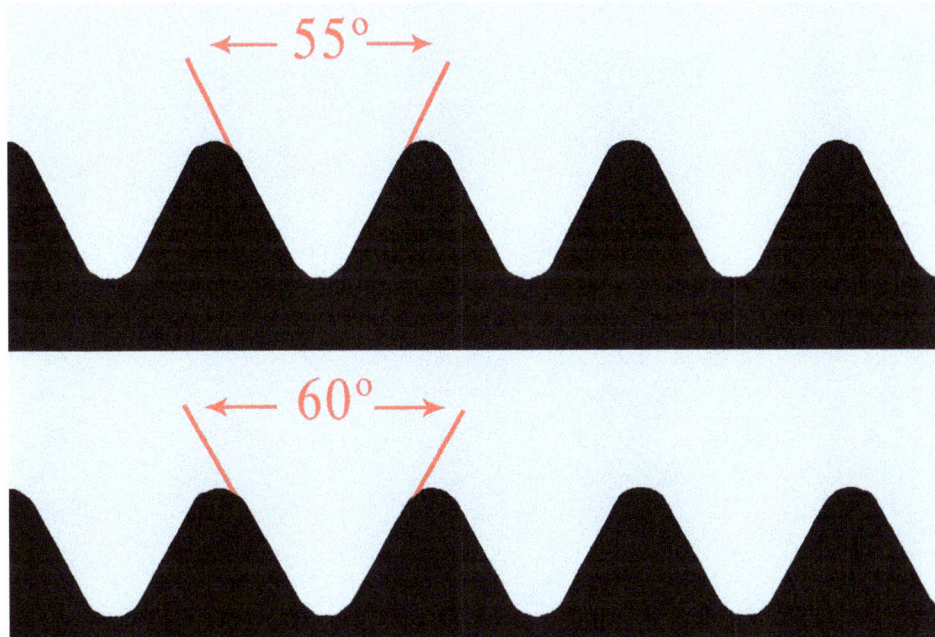

People think that Triumphs are assembled with Whitworth fasteners. In truth, the pre-unit bikes use mostly CEI (Cycle Engineers' Institute) Fasteners. The Whitworth system uses a 55 degree angle (as shown), while the CEI fasteners use 60 degree angle, thus the two systems can't be interchanged.

Chapter Seven

Complete Assembly

1959 - The First Bonneville

The 1959 Bonneville is not only the first Bonnie, it's also a pretty unique model, with parts that were only used on this one model. Unlike the '60 and later Bonnevilles with their trim fenders and stand-alone headlights, the '59 Bonneville used valanced fenders and a complete headlight nacelle.

The fact is, Ed Turner and crew based the Bonneville on their fastest road bike of the period, the T110. As Garry Chitwood explains, "The things that separate the Bonnie from the T110 are the head; the twin carbs with remote float bowl, and the three gallon tank."

Restoring a '59 Bonneville can be tough, not only is it a pre-unit bike, but it also uses a number of parts unique to this year and model.

"The problem areas I run into when I'm restoring one of these first-year Bonnevilles are the gas tank, fenders and the nacelle pieces. The nacelle is made up of three pieces, the left, right and the top. All that tin is pretty tough to find. The accessory box and oil tank are hard to find in good condition too. The ones you get are usually all banged up, or the mounting tabs broke off so someone made a homemade tab and welded it to the oil tank. The later bikes used rubber-mounted oil tanks and accessory boxes, so they stood up to the vibration better."

"This particular bike started out as a frame and a set of cases with matching numbers. There was no sheet metal. So we had to find everything else. The heads are almost impossible to find, so are the carbs. We built the entire bike out of parts. The nacelle pieces came from the UK.

"It makes a big difference if the bike was all together once, when you take that nacelle apart, you know it will go back together. When you start with a bunch of new parts, it doesn't always work out. Those parts have never been together before and they don't always like to go together. With a bike like this there are a lot of fitment issues."

"For this bike the gas tank required a lot of work. The mounting holes at the front of the tank are supposed to be 5/16X26, but they were taped out to a 3/8-inch thread. We had to cut out the bottom plate, weld in new nuts of the correct size and pitch, and then weld the plate back onto the tank. On the top of the tank the parcel grid mounting holes were stripped out too. You can cut those plugs out of the tank and weld in new ones, but we just brazed the holes closed and then drilled and tapped the holes. And there were plenty of small dents we had to fill, as well. The rear fender must have come off a T110 with a set of saddlebags, because it was full of holes from where the bags were mounted."

"You know, when you look at the paint on these early Bonnevilles, no two are alike, some have a green tint and some are more gray. We bought the paint for this bike from Don Hutchinson, out of Wakeville, Massachusetts, he mixes it up special."

"This bike was a hard one to build, because we had to find and repair all those parts. For someone doing this without our resources, it would have been more efficient to just buy a nicer bike as a starting point, or to purchase one from the '60s, so parts wouldn't be so hard to come by."

Here are all the components for our '59 frame, the front section, rear section, and swingarm.

I'm installing a 5mm spacer between the swingarm and frame...

...we install the shim on the right side, using a hammer and punch to carefully tap it into place. As mentioned before, there is no spacer on the other side.

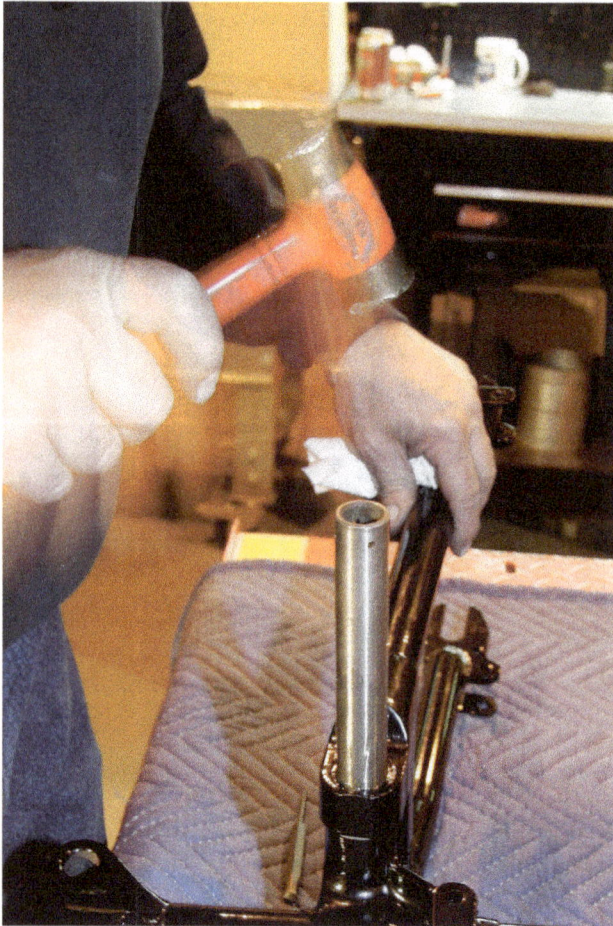

With the frame on its side it's time to tap in the spindle bushing.

The assembled frame. We like to have the frame components powder coated for durability.

Installing the drivetrain begins with the transmission as shown.

Once the pivot shaft and swing arm are in place, I install the spindle bushing and end caps.

With the transmission in position, we can install the bottom stud for the transmission.

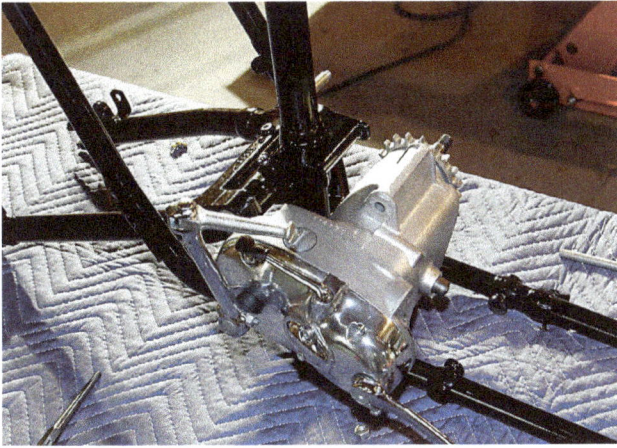

Transmission in the rear section of the frame, complete.

Now we can set the engine in place...

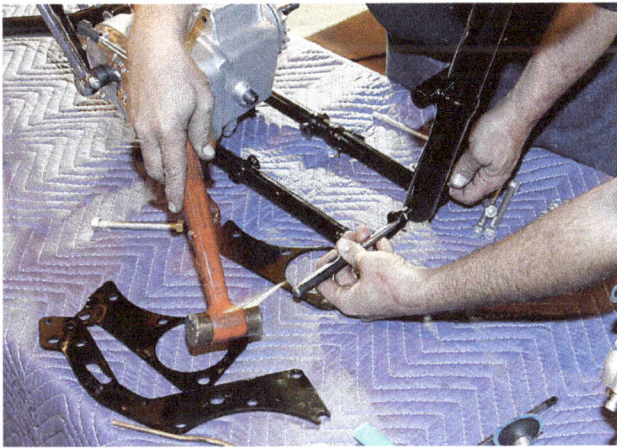

Next, we align the front lower section of the frame, prior to installing the left and right front engine plates.

...and get the left and right transmission, and engine plates, positioned correctly.

Sometimes there's too much powder coat on the edges of the holes, and you need to clean them out with a round file.

These are the 2 distance tubes used between the rear engine plates.

With the transmission and engine plates in place we can put in the bottom distance tube between the plates.

Here you can see the left side of the transmission and mounting plates.

This progress shot shows the complete bottom end and the transmission installed in the frame.

Time to install the generator we rebuilt.

The primary chain tension is adjusted with the gearbox-adjuster assembly shown here.

The generator slides into place through the front engine mounting plates, note the cork gasket in position on the front of the generator.

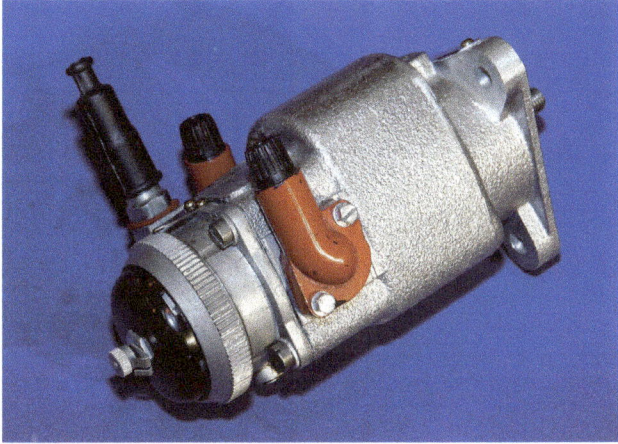

Luckily we have a NOS magneto for this project.

The complete layout of the primary side components.

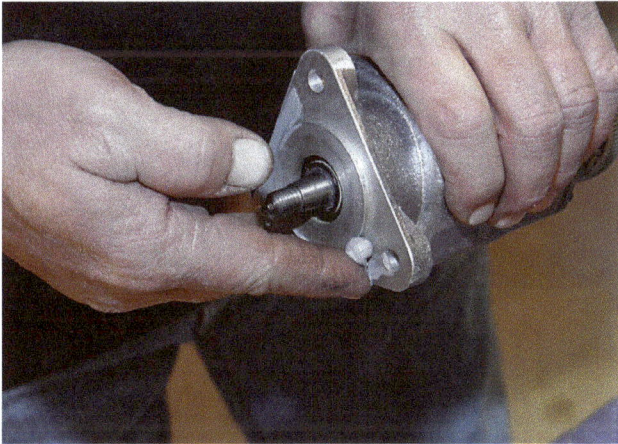

Before installing the magneto, I apply a bead of grey Permatex to the mounting face.

Before installing the inner primary cover, put a bead of grey Permatex on the left side engine case.

With Permatex in place, I can install the new, old-stock, magneto.

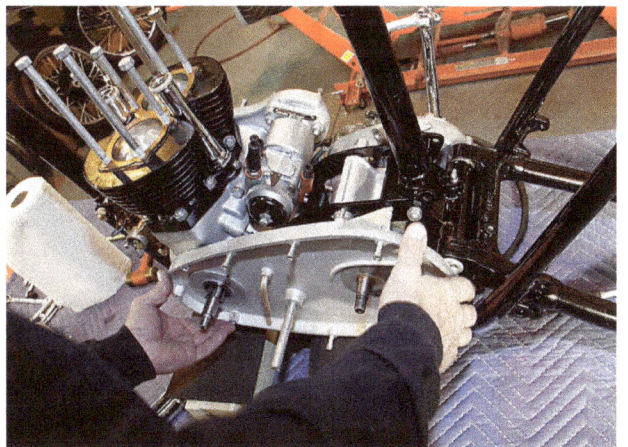

Now I can install the inner primary cover.

Progress shot of the left side engine and transmission, note the "seal" on the transmission shaft.

Now I put the 22 tooth sprocket gear on the left side crankshaft.

A flat file can be used to trim off the burrs on the key.

With the sprocket gear in place, it's time to install the flat key...

...followed by the spacer as shown.

Install the tab washer and engine sprocket nut for the primary side.

Next, grease up the hub for the clutch basket.

And install the roller sets, which include 20 roller bearings for the clutch hub.

Here's our clutch basket before assembly.

Now I slide the clutch basket over the roller bearings.

We use grease to hold the shock absorber body clutch bolts in place, as shown.

The cup washer for the clutch basket is next...

With clutch hub bolts in place, install the center shock absorber body over the clutch hub.

...followed by the tab washer...

With clutch basket complete, we can install it on the mainshaft.

...and finally the clutch security nut.

Progress shot of the clutch basket completely installed.

We use a primary chain breaker to remove unneeded links.

We use a home-made tool to hold the clutch hub while the clutch security nut is tightened to 25 to 30 ft. lbs.

Like almost any other chain, the primary chain has a master link.

The primary chain comes raw, and needs to be cut to the correct length.

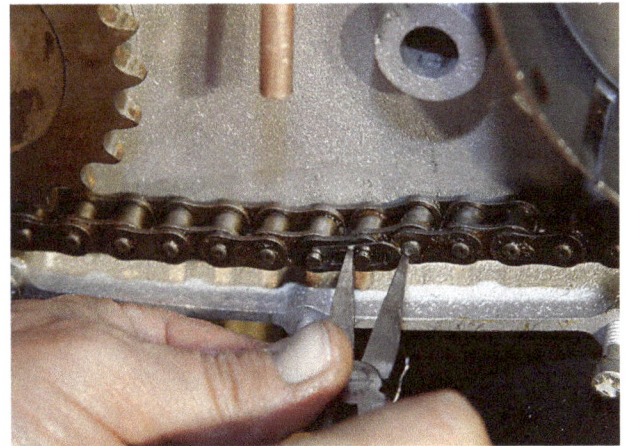

We install master link as shown, note the direction of travel.

We adjust the position of the transmission, and the chain tension, as shown.

Before installing the bonded plates, be sure to coat them in oil.

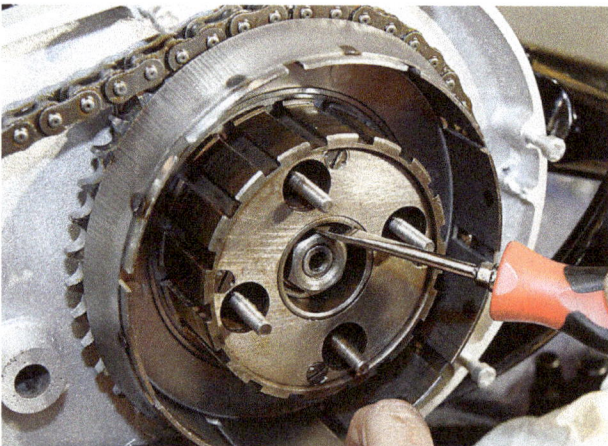

Once the security nut is tight, bend the tab washer over to lock the nut in place.

Alternate steel driving plates and bonded plates. You should start and finish with a steel driving plate.

Install the driving plates and bonded plates in the clutch basket. Note: there are 5 bonded plates and 6 plain driving plates (steel).

Here's the assembly after the last steel plate is installed.

Now install the pressure plate to the clutch basket...

Once installed, tighten the clutch spring nuts. Note: tighten the clutch spring nuts until they are flush with the clutch stud.

...followed by the clutch push rod.

Using an impact wrench, tighten the engine sprocket nut.

Install the clutch springs on the pressure plate.

After the engine sprocket nut has been tightened, fold over the tab washer.

Here's the oil restrictor screw for the primary chain case.

The filler plug and gasket.

Before putting the outer primary in place, run a thin bead of grey Permatex along the mating surface.

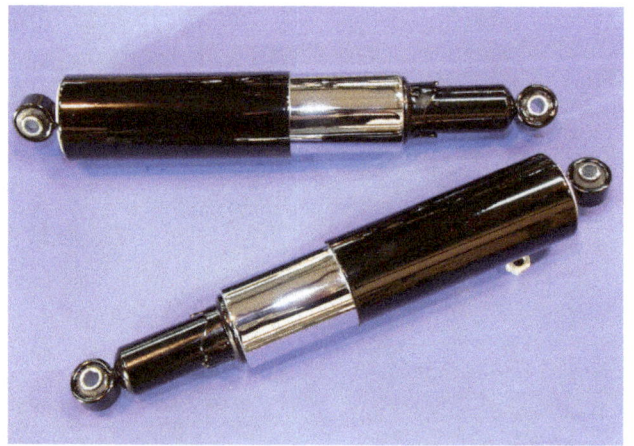

Chassis time, these are the completely rebuilt rear shocks for our Bonneville .

Then slip the cover in place and tighten down the screws. Remember, these aren't standard Phillips head screws.

At this point the engine and transmission are installed in the frame and the whole thing is starting to look like a motorcycle.

Installation of the rear shocks is next.

Outer timing chest cover and patent plate. New plates are still available.

When in doubt, always stop and clean the threads before installing a bolt. This 5/16X26 tap is being used to chase the threads for the passenger pegs.

Next comes the brake spindle.

Install the patent plate to outer timing chest cover as shown, driving down the special rivets with a small hammer.

Sliding the C clip under the bolt-head for the auto-advance assembly.

Auto advance in its original position, as seen from the timing side.

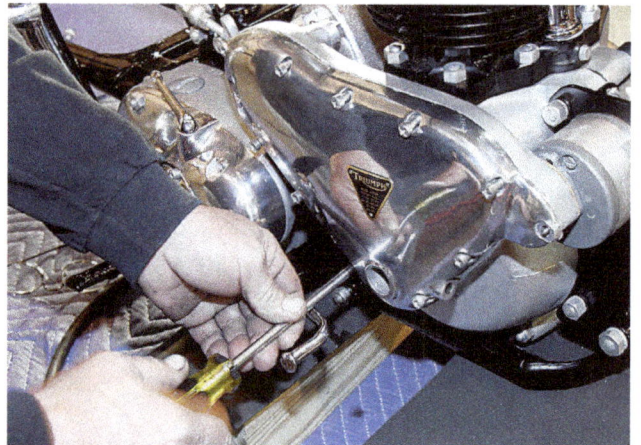

Once the timing side is complete, I put on the timing chest cover.

With the auto-advance in place on the magneto shaft, it's time to tighten the drive nut.

Layout of the top and bottom triple tree, with the damper, for the '59 Bonneville.

The bottom race being pushed onto the bottom lug with a piece of pipe of the correct diameter.

Putting the top race in place for the '59 Bonneville. Note: there are 20 of the 1/4 inch ball bearings.

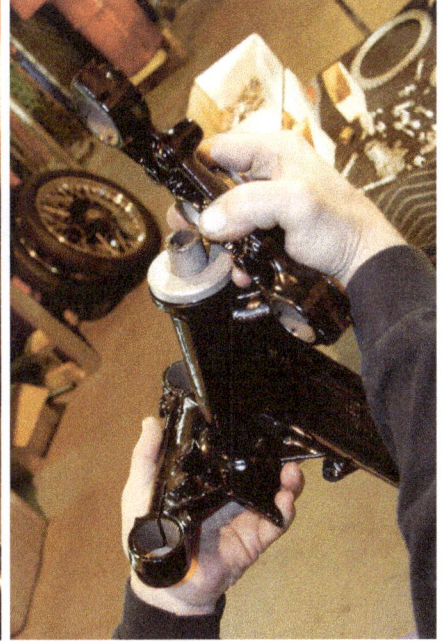

With the bearings in place, we put the top and bottom lug into position.

The top and bottom lug installed.

The adjuster sleeve and friction disc ready to be installed.

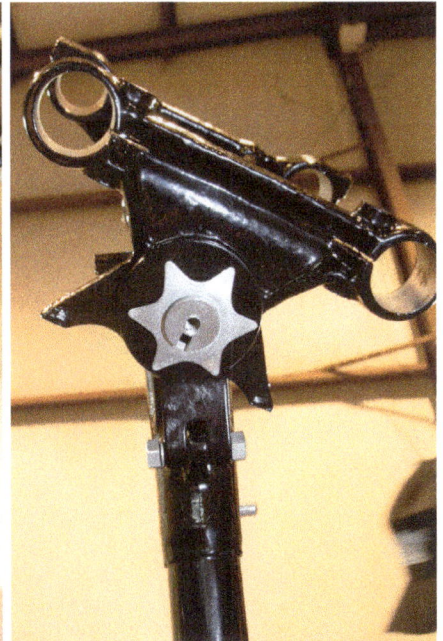

The friction disc in place on the bottom lug.

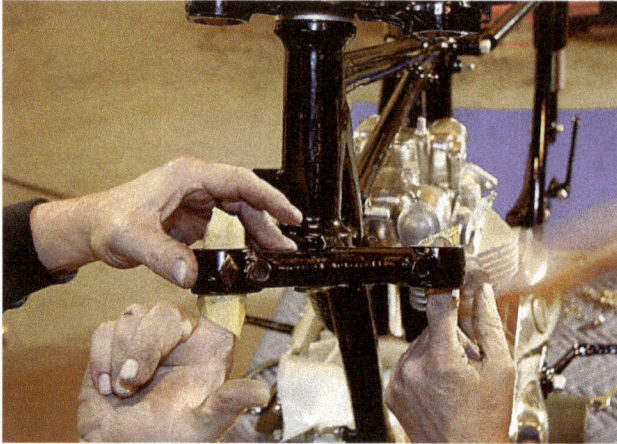

The top and bottom lug have been installed, now use 180 grit sand paper, to sand out extra powder coat paint in the fork-tube holes.

Left, right, and top components for the headlight nacelle.

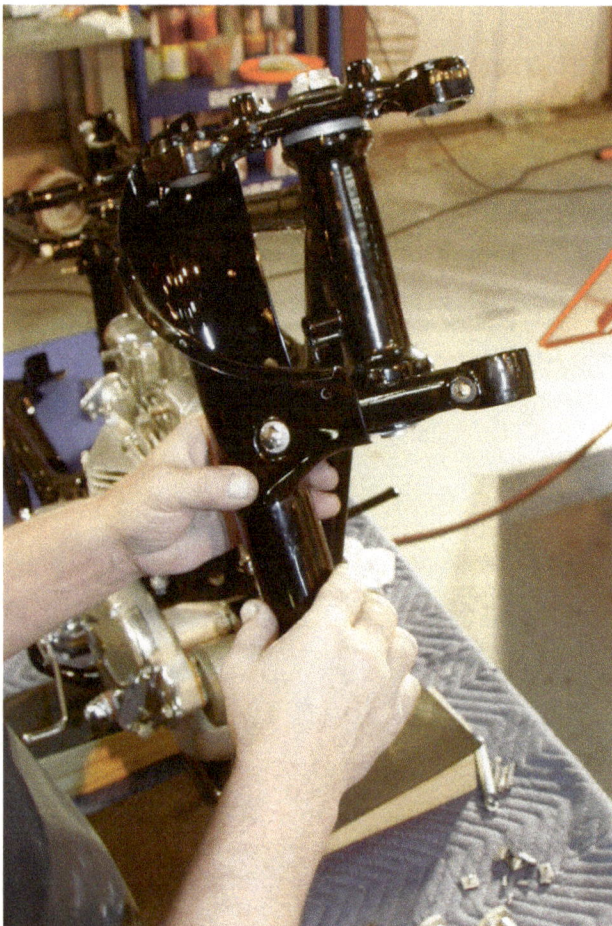

Next, install the bottom piece for the left side of the nacelle.

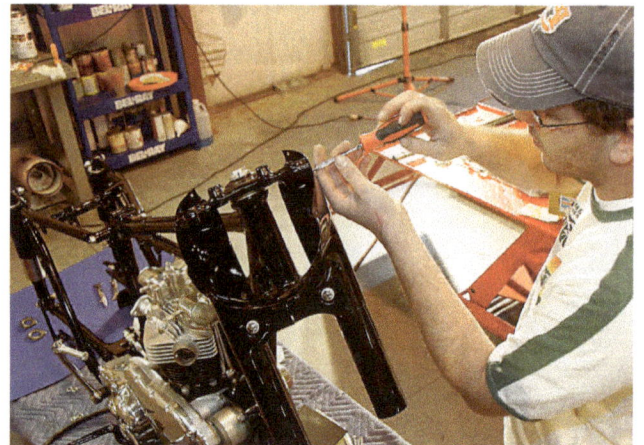

Left, right, and bottom nacelle components installed.

Oil the fork tubes before you slide them through the bottom and top lugs.

GENTLY tap on the bottom of the fork tube, using a piece of fiberglass or wood to work the fork tube into place.

Now tighten up the cap assembly nut, as shown.

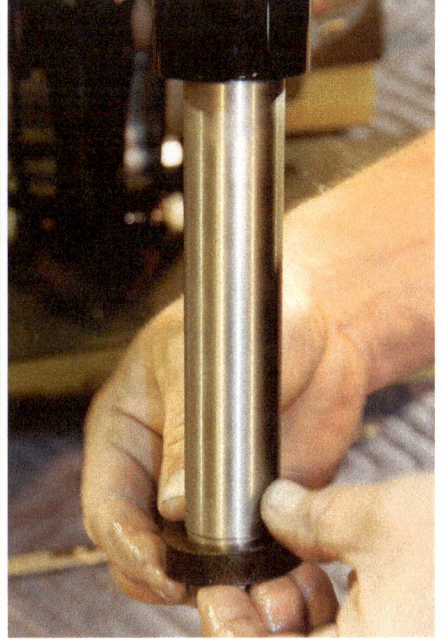

Next, push up the sponge rubber washer over the fork tube. Note: this spaces out the bottom nacelle leg.

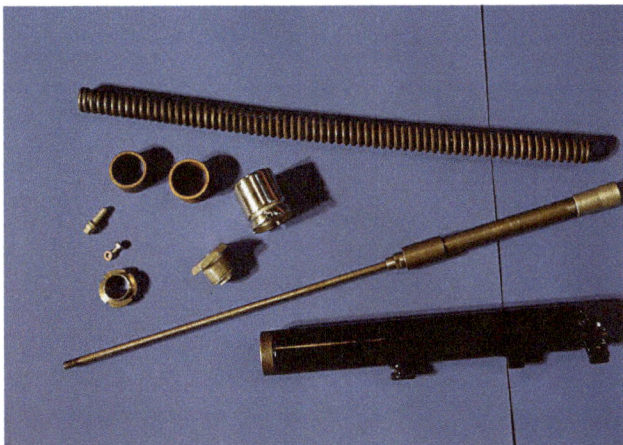

The lower leg, restrictor tubes and seal holder.

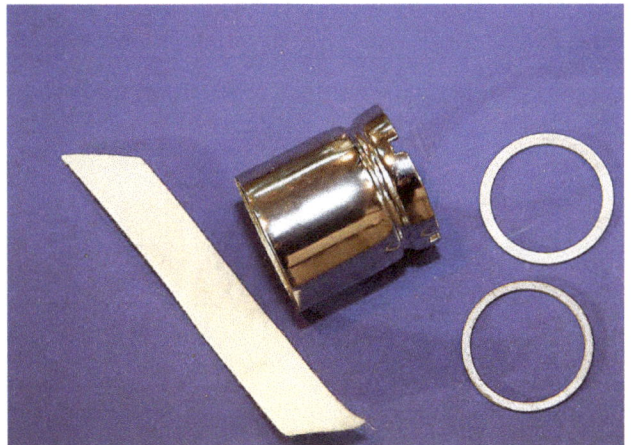

The seal holder, washer, and felt seal for the fork tube.

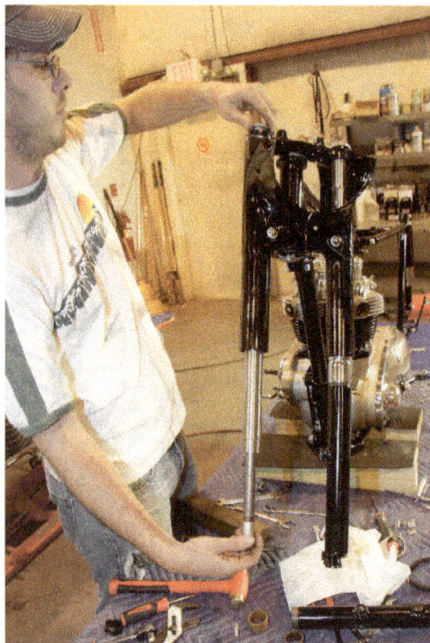

Slide down the restrictor rod on the left side.

Left: Putting on the top and bottom fork bushings. Right: With the fork bushings in place, slide up the lower fork leg.

Push down the top fork bushing into the lower leg.

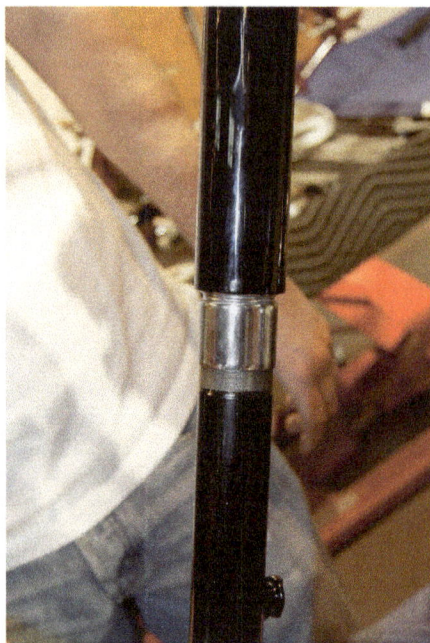

Here's the lower leg being screwed into the seal holder.

Tightening the flange bolt to the bottom of the restrictor rod with a small socket as shown.

This is the lower leg with the flange bolt and drain plug installed correctly.

Lower nacelle and lower legs installed.

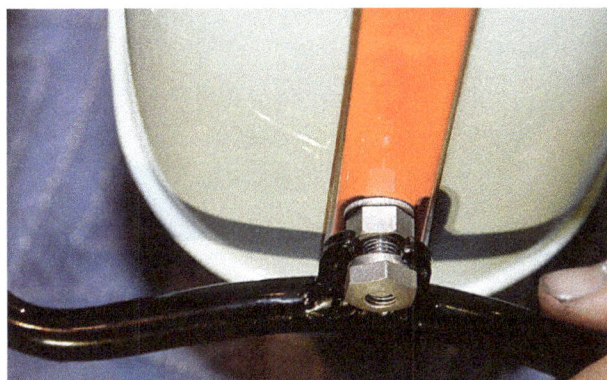

With the front fender in place, add the bottom stay and connect to the back of the front fender, as shown.

With help from James, I can now install the rear fender to '59 Bonneville.

Once the lower legs are in place, put on the front fender for the '59. Note: BE VERY CAREFUL that you don't scratch the paint.

Here's our Bonneville at the end of day 3.

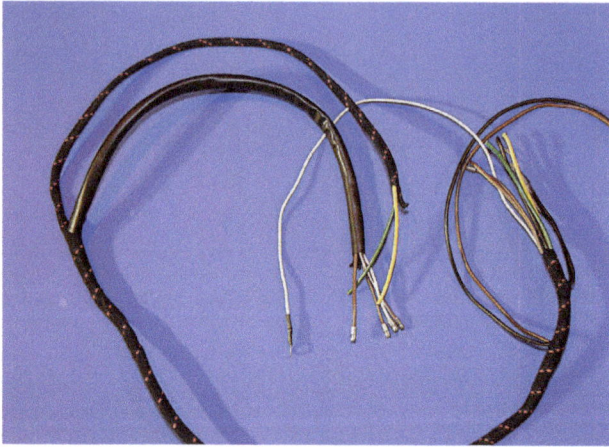

The main wiring harness for our '59 Bonneville.

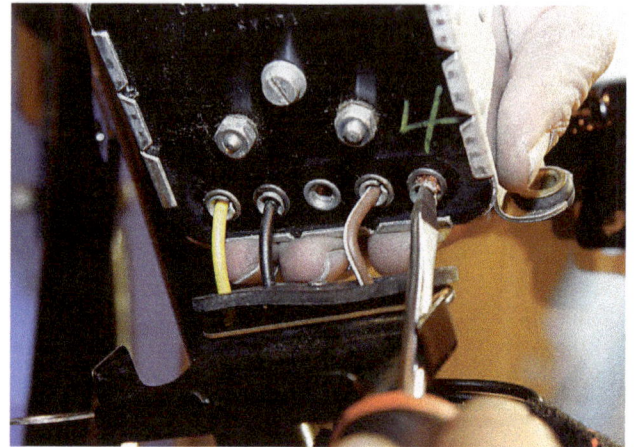

Using a screw driver, connect the terminals to the voltage regulator.

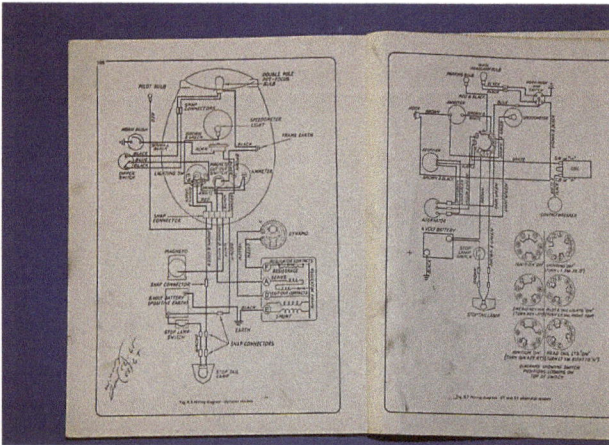

It's a good idea to have a diagram available.

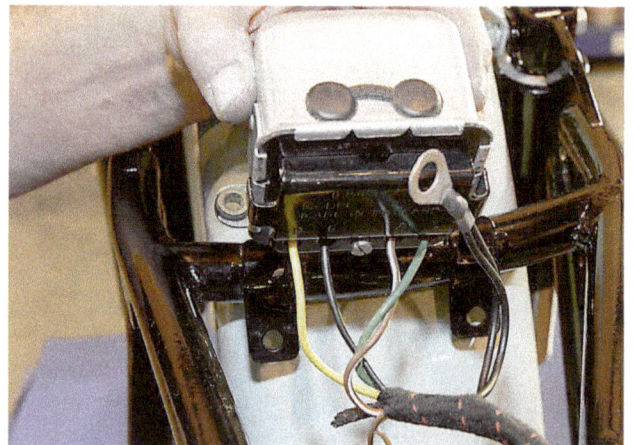

With the voltage regulator wired we can now bolt it to the rear frame section.

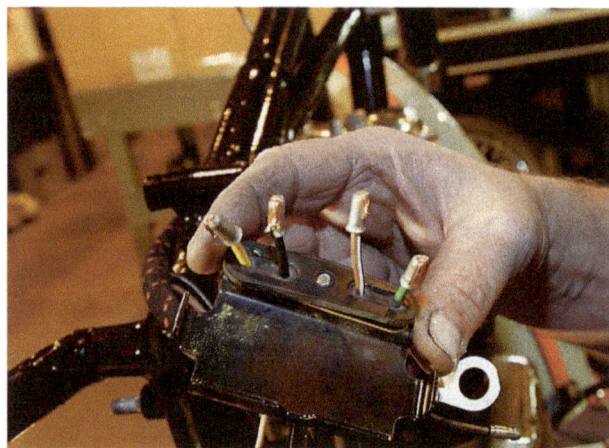

You can see the wiring for the RB/107 voltage regulator.

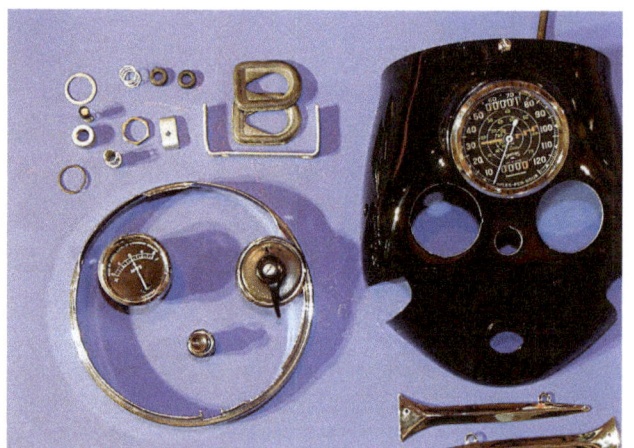

Top nacelle layout: with amp meter, switches, trim and speedo.

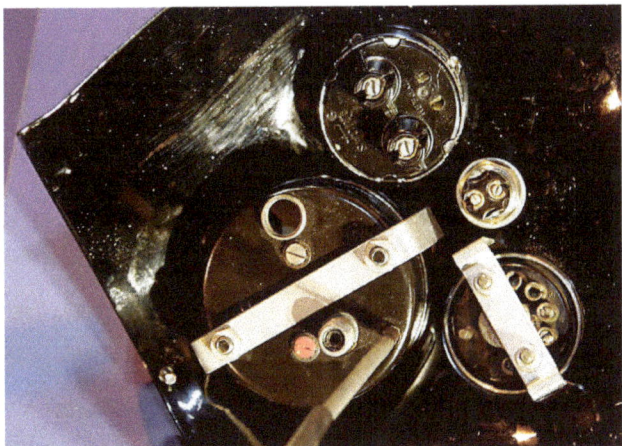

The inside of the top nacelle with the ammeter, kill button, lighting switch and speedo completed.

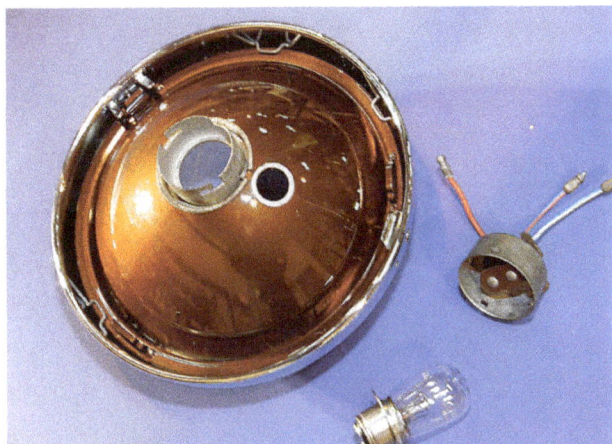

The headlight bulb and socket.

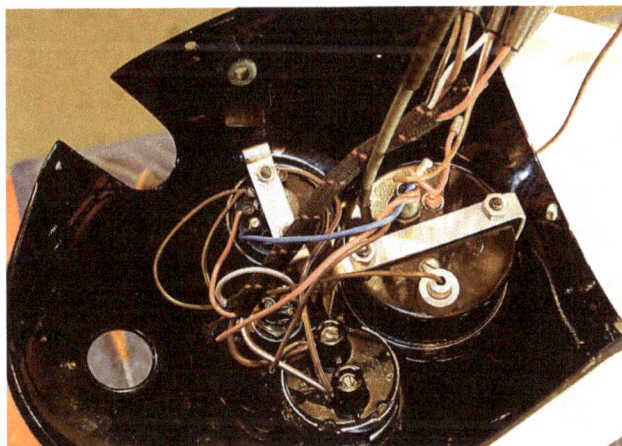

Completed wiring for the top nacelle.

Connecting the headlight to the inner chrome ring.

Connecting the top nacelle to the bottom left, and right, nacelle halves.

The generator installed, with leads ready to be hooked up.

'59 Bonneville after day 4.

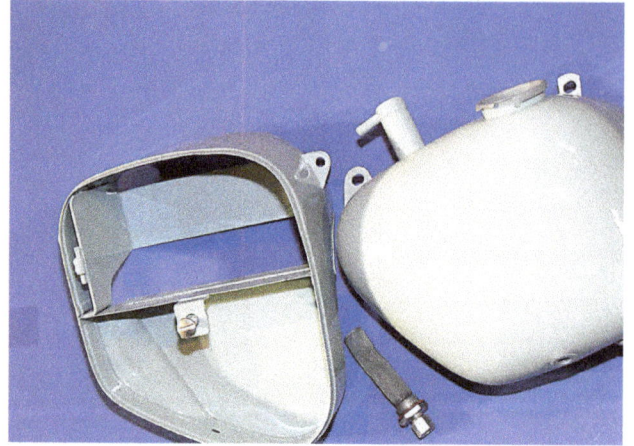
The oil tank and accessory box cover.

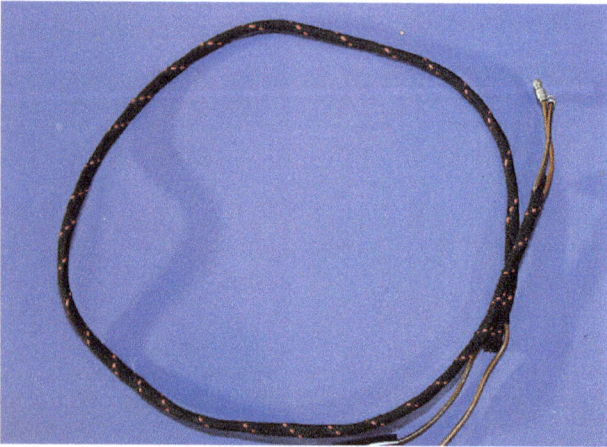
The rear taillight lead wires.

Install the 5/16 nut for the oil tank top bracket.

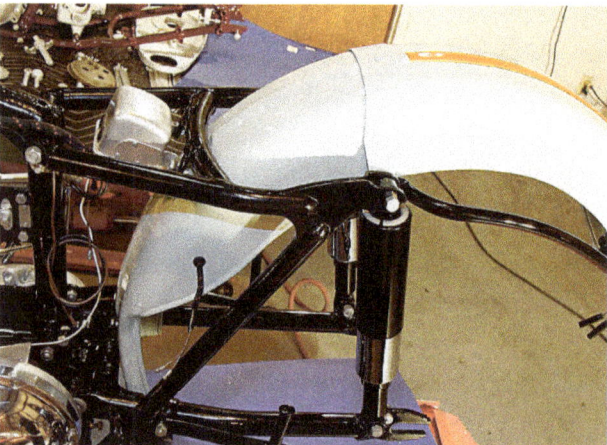
The rear taillight lead wires routed through the front part of the rear fender.

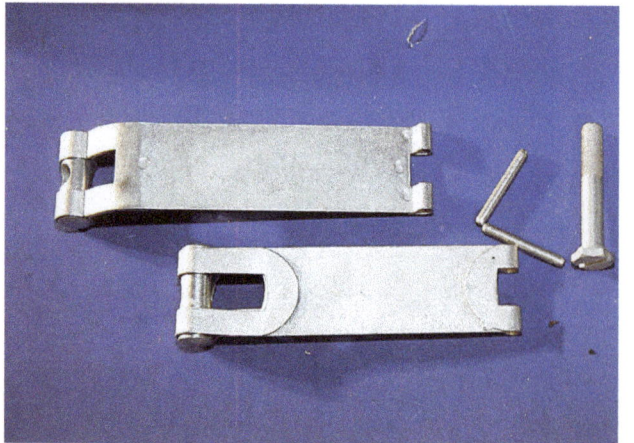
The battery box straps with hinge pins.

Accessory box installed on our '59 Bonnie.

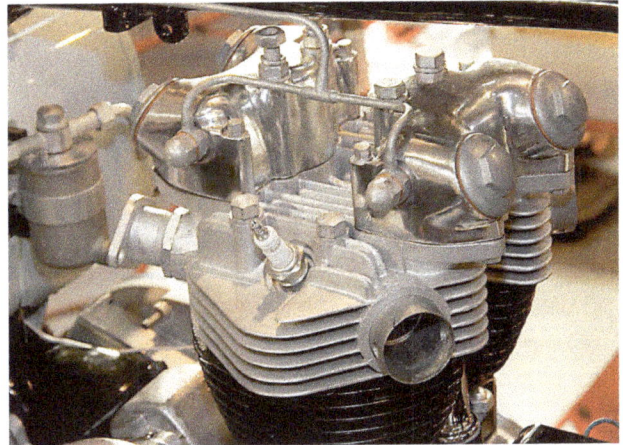
The top end oil feed pipe connected to the rocker boxes.

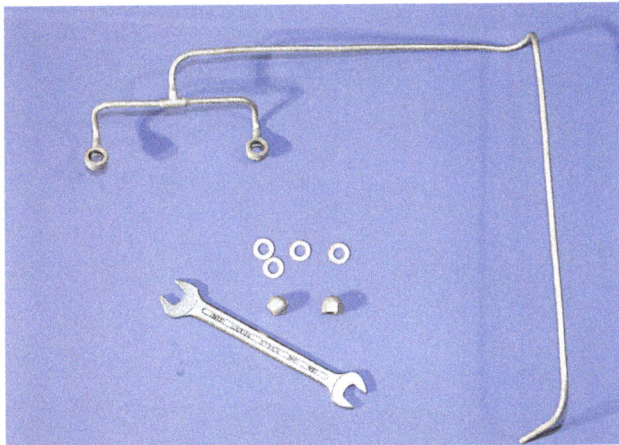
Here's the oil feed pipe for rocker box...

The remote float bowl & parts.

...which needs to be shortened slightly to the correct length.

The completed remote float bowl attached to back of down tube.

The front brakes, brake cover and assorted parts.

The front wheel installed in the lower legs.

Adding on the front cover plate to front hub.

Now tap in the dust cover for the rear hub.

With the wheel complete, install the front wheel to the '59 Bonneville.

The '59 rear wheel complete with bearings and dust cover.

Installing the rear brake hub.

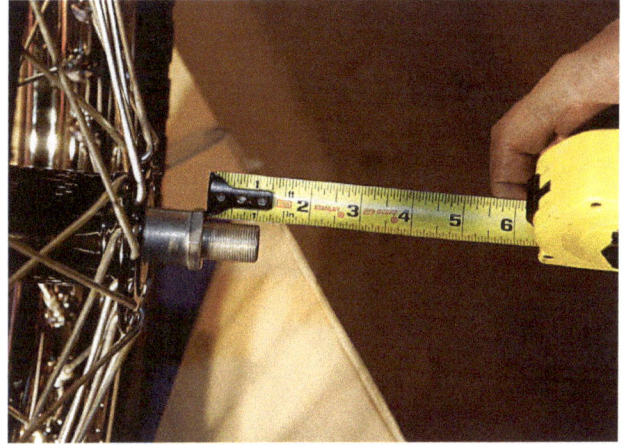

The rear hub and axle complete. Space the axle equally on both sides using a measuring tape. Note: general rule of thumb is 1 to 1-1/8 inches on each side.

Once the hub is in place, install and tighten the hub bolts.

You need a helper to support the bike while the rear wheel assembly is rolled into place.

With the axle in place, put on the axle nuts.

Install the rear brake pedal spindle.

1. Our '59 Bonneville midway through day 5.

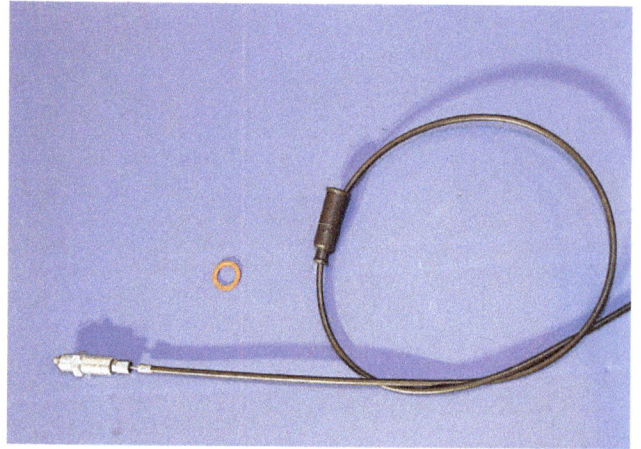

2. The cable advance with cable, nut, and washer.

3. Installing the cable advance for the magneto.

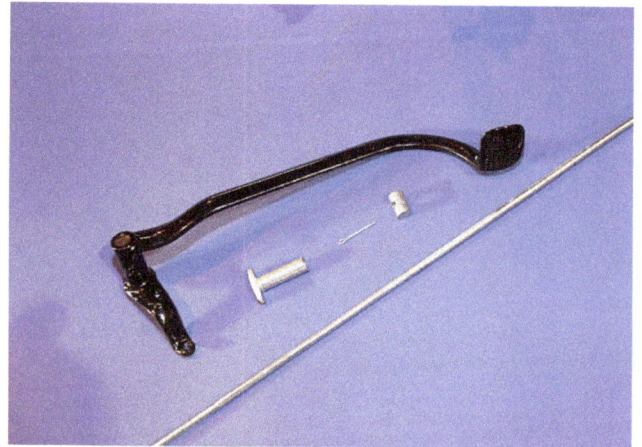

4. Brake pedal and brake rod...

5. ...which are installed on the bike as shown.

With Danny's help I'm installing the exhaust pipes. The inset photo shows the correct front pipe brackets.

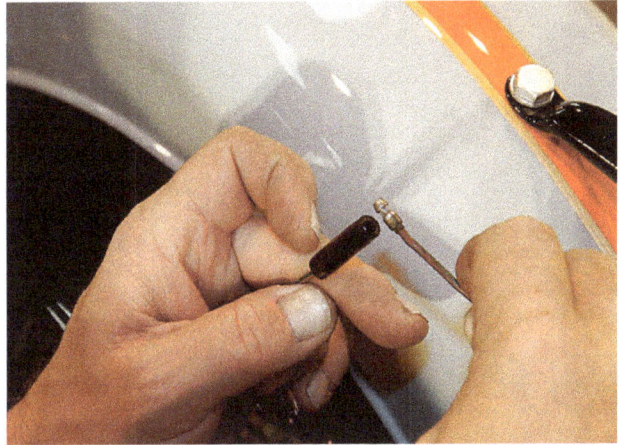

Wire the 2 leads from the light assembly to the taillight harness seen earlier in the assembly sequence.

The rear taillight assembly.

We are ready to wire the generator for the '59 Bonneville. Note: the 2 leads are green and yellow.

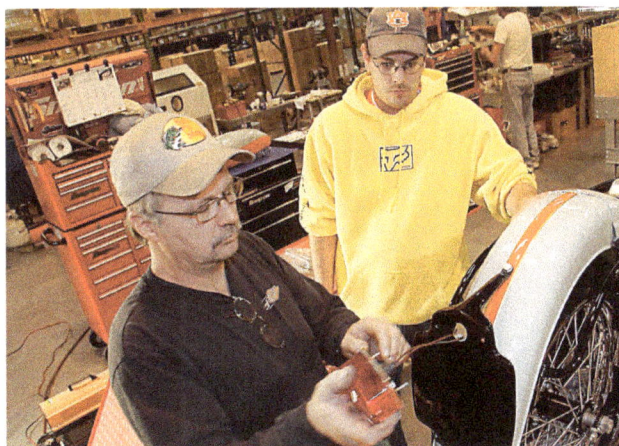

Once the taillight assembly is wired, it's time to install the light to the number plate.

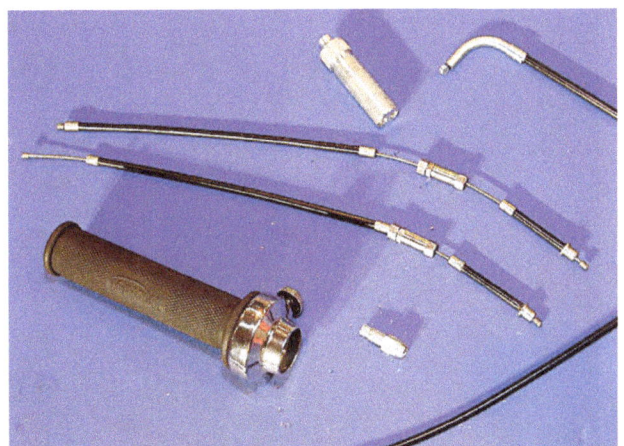

The throttle assembly and cables.

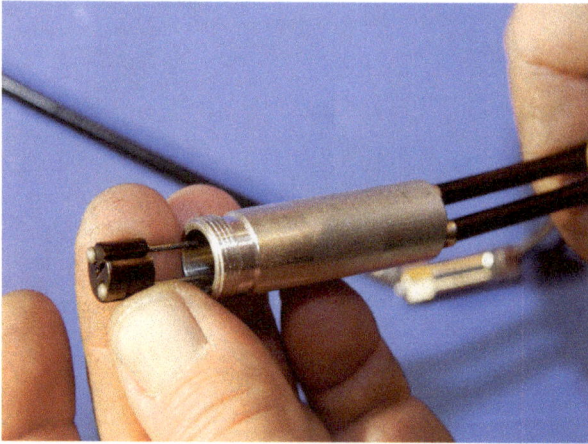

To start, connect the junction box to the throttle cables as shown.

Install the twist grip cable to the throttle assembly. Make sure you catch the nipple in the slot inside the throttle.

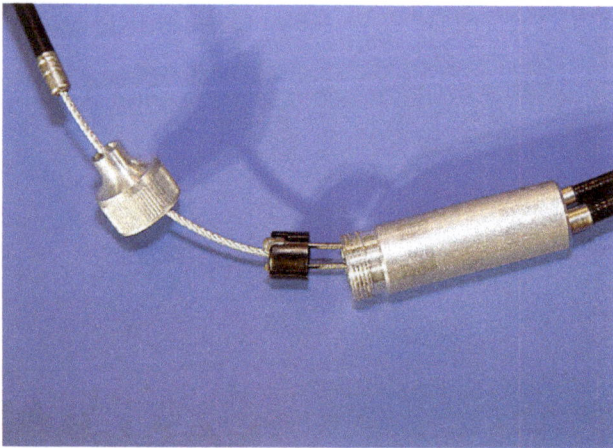

Here you see the junction box, 2 carburetor cables, and the throttle cable.

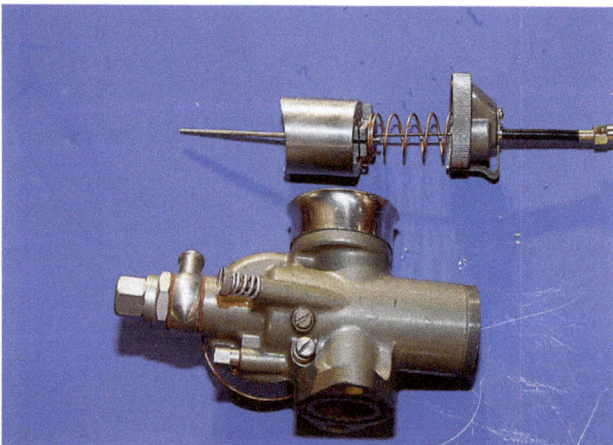

We used new/old stock carburetors for this build.

Carburetor cable complete with throttle valve, needle and spring.

With the cable attached, slide the throttle valve into the carburetor.

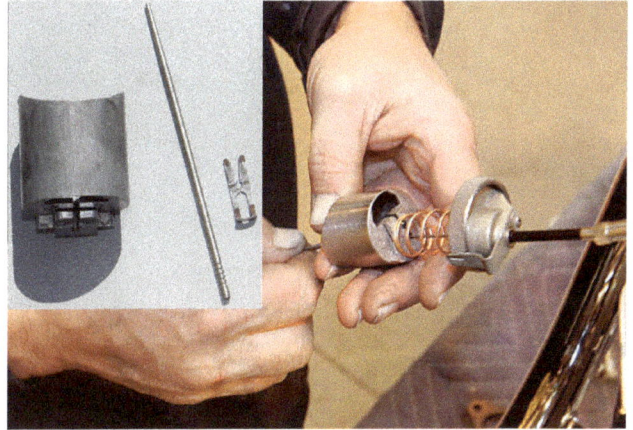

Here I'm pushing the throttle needle through the throttle valve into the middle position. Inset photo from another assembly gives a closeup of the needle and clip.

Adjust cable adjusters for the carburetor. There should be 1/16 inch of play in the housing.

The right side carburetor shown complete.

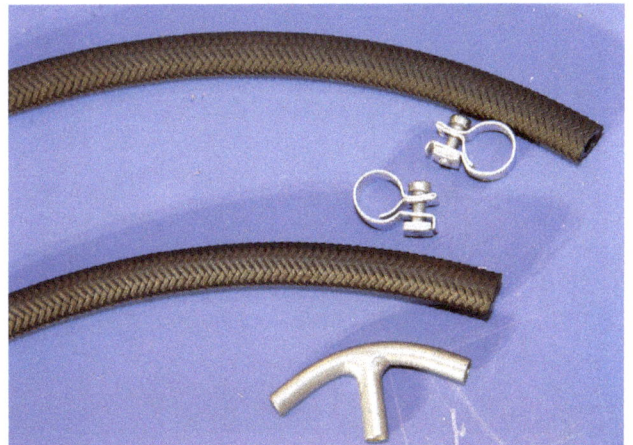

We like to use 5/16 inch herring bone line for the fuel line.

Here's the routing of the bottom fuel lines from remote float bowl to left and right carburetors.

Here are the finished oil lines from oil the tank to the oil feed pipe.

The left and right carburetor as shown, completed and installed.

The '59 gas tank ready for chrome accessories.

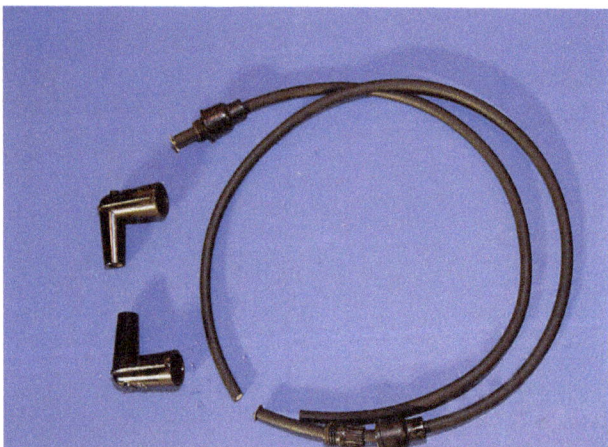

The magneto leads with the correct KLG lug caps.

The gas tank mounted to '59 frame with the tank rubber plates installed.

Here's how I like to route the gas line to the petcock.

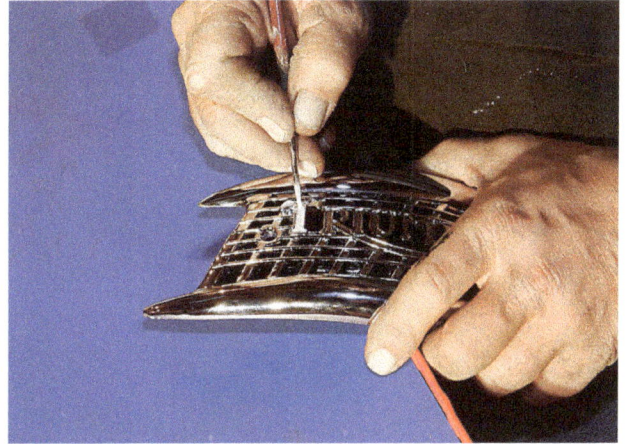

Use white paint to brush in the "Triumph" script for the badge.

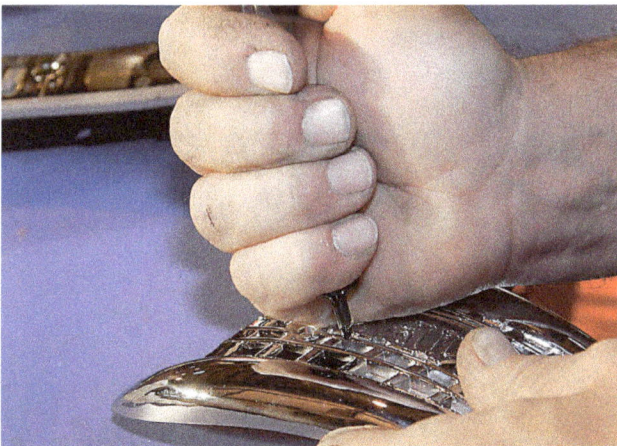

To paint the tank badge, fill the tank badge blocks with paint using a syringe. This makes it much easier to neatly paint each of the blocks on the badge.

Completely painted badge, it's all in the details.

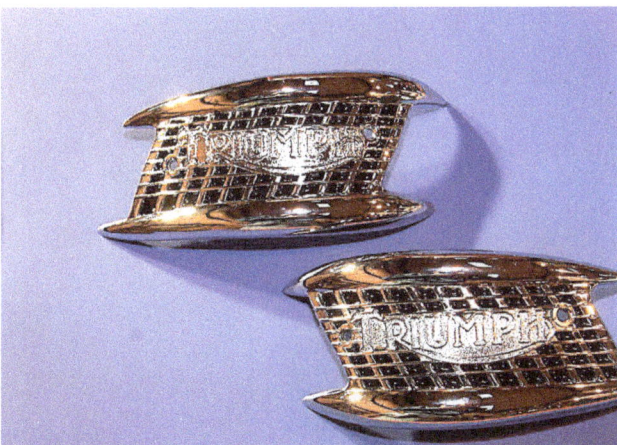

The left and right badges after the individual blocks have been filled with black paint.

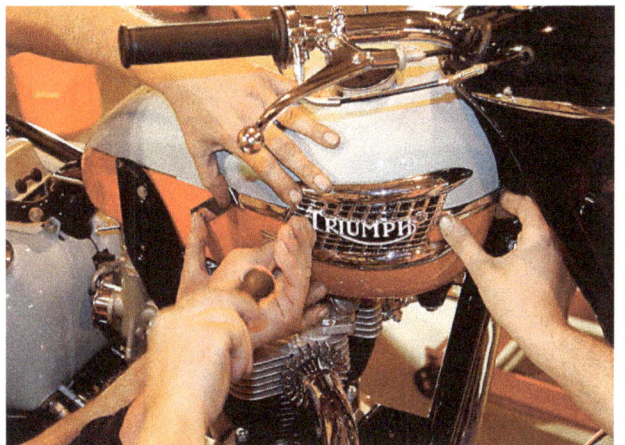

The badge and styling strips being applied to the gas tank.

After installing the center styling strip on the gas tank, it's time to put the package grid on the tank.

Once the chain is assembled to the right length, you can adjust the rear wheel using the axle adjusters.

One of the last things we do is install the rear seat for the '59 Bonneville.

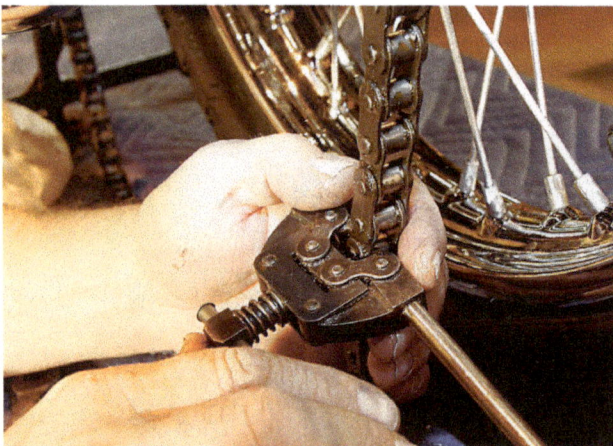

After measuring the rear chain, use a chain breaker to remove unnecessary chain links.

End of day 5, one complete '59 Bonneville.

A '59 Bonneville can make a great, though challenging, restoration project. The tank, carbs and cylinder head are unique to this year. Most of the other parts are shared with the T110, which means they aren't exactly commonplace. Before buying a really rough Bonneville, or any old Triumph for that matter, consider the cost of finding and repairing all those missing or damaged parts.

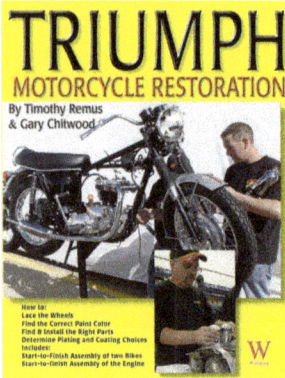

TRIUMPH MOTORCYCLE RESTORATION

As popular as the Triumph Twins were in the 60s and 70s, they are quite possibly more popular now. The new book from Wolfgang Publications offers complete start-to-finish assembly and restoration sequences on two Triumph Twins, a 1963 Bonneville and a 1969 Bonneville. Also included is the start-to-finish assembly of the 1969 engine and transmission. Rather than try to describe the miniscule differences that often separated one year from another, this book offers a color gallery with left and right side views of all significant models from 1959 to 1970. With over 450 color photos, Triumph Restoration offers 144 pages of hard-core how-to help for anyone who wants to repair or restore their own Triumph twin.

Seven Chapters   144 Pages $29.95   Over 450 photos, 100% color

AMERICAN POLICE MOTORCYCLES - REVISED

American Police Motorcycle is the newest title from Wolfgang Publications, well known publisher of motorcycle titles. See Harley-Davidson VLs from 1931 decked out with radio and lights, and row upon row of Indian Police-Specials ready to leave the Springfield factory.

Over 200 black and white images, many supplied by the various police departments and never before published, give this book a fresh perspective on a unique group of American motorcycles. More than just great photos, this new book also contains first person anecdotes as told by the cycle-cops themselves.

Compiled by author Buck Lovell, this book is a must for anyone who appreciates American two wheelers. 144 pages. Over 200 black and white images.

Seven Chapters   144 Pages $24.95   Over 200 B&W photos,

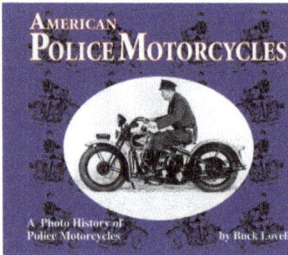

ULTIMATE TRIUMPH COLLECTION

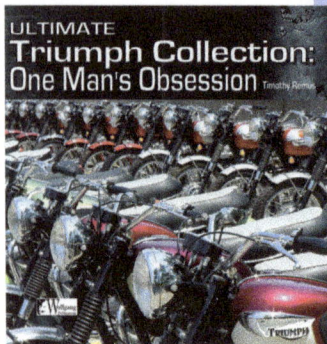

Ultimate Triumph Collection presents nearly 80 perfect Triumphs, from early singles to an immaculate Speed Twin, from an iconic 1953 Blackbird to a pair of 1970 Bonnevilles, all belonging to one man. What started as a restoration project on an old motorcycle twenty years ago grew into a small collection of nice Triumphs.

The meat of this book is the photos of those very bikes, presented one bike per page, each with a short caption. Photos need context; collections aren't built in a vacuum. Chapters one and two provide a history of both the collection and the man who built it. Most collections contain a few gems, and those bright diamonds fill the final chapter: The T110 with Swallow side car, the ultra rare 350cc 3H, the '38 Speed Twin, and the new first-year Bonneville.

Ultimate Triumph Collection is an inside look at One Man's Obsession - one man's successful quest to assemble and own the world's best personal collection of the world's most beautiful motorcycles.

10X10 inches, hard cover, printed on art-quality paper. Best selection of Triumphs you'll ever see.

Four Chapters   144 Pages $49.95   Over 300 photos, 100% color HARDCOVER

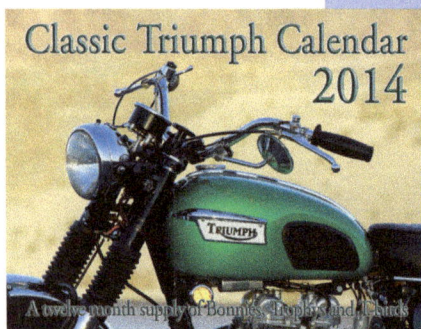

CLASSIC TRIUMPH CALENDAR

From Bonnevilles to T110s and Tigers, the Classic Triumph Calendar includes something for every one. Printed on heavy art quality paper and measuring a full sixteen inches horizontal, these pure motorcycle prints will turn into posters when the year is past. Photographed by Timothy Remus, this collection of Triumphs stand as testimony to the design genius of Edward Turner and the staff at The Triumph Corporation. Available from Baxter Cycle or Wolfgang Publications.

$19.95

Wolfgang Publication Titles

For a current list visit our website at www.wolfpub.com

ILLUSTRATED HISTORY

Ultimate Triumph Collection	$49.95

BIKER BASICS

Custom Bike Building Basics	$24.95
Sportster/Buell Engine Hop-Up Guide	$24.95
Sheet Metal Fabrication Basics	$24.95
How to Fix American T-Twin Motorcycles	$27.95

COMPOSITE GARAGE

Composite Materials Handbook #1	$27.95
Composite Materials Handbook #2	$27.95
Composite Materials Handbook #3	$27.95

HOT ROD BASICS

Hot Rod Wiring	$27.95
How to Chop Tops	$24.95
How to Air Condition Your Hot Rod	$24.95

MOTORCYCLE RESTORATION SERIES

Triumph Restoration - Unit 650cc	$29.95
Triumph MC Restoration Pre-Unit	$29.95

CUSTOM BUILDER SERIES

How to Build A Café Racer	$27.95
Advanced Custom Motorcycle Wiring - Revised	$27.95
How to Build an Old Skool Bobber Sec Ed	$27.95
How To Build The Ultimate V-Twin Motorcycle	$24.95
Advanced Custom Motorcycle Assembly & Fabrication	$27.95
How to Build a Cheap Chopper	$27.95

SHEET METAL

Advanced Sheet Metal Fabrication	$27.95
Ultimate Sheet Metal Fabrication	$24.95
Sheet Metal Bible	$29.95

AIR SKOOL SKILLS

Airbrush Bible	$29.95
How Airbrushes Work	$24.95

PAINT EXPERT

How To Airbrush, Pinstripe & Goldleaf	$27.95
Kosmoski's	
New Kustom Painting Secrets	$27.95
Pro Pinstripe Techniques	$27.95
Advanced Pinstripe Art	$27.95

TATTOO U Series

Into The Skin The Ultimate Tattoo Sourcebook	$34.95
Tattoo Sketch Book	$32.95
American Tattoos	$27.95
Advanced Tattoo Art	$27.95
Tattoo Bible Book One	$27.95
Tattoo Bible Book Two	$27.95
Tattoo Bible Book Three	$27.95

NOTEWORTHY

American Police Motorcycles - Revised	$24.95

LIFESTYLE

Bean're — Motorcycle Nomad	$18.95
George The Painter	$18.95
The Colorful World of Tattoo Models	$34.95

Sources

Baxter Cycle
400 Lincoln
Marne, IA
712 781 2351
www.baxtercycle.com

Chitwood, Garry
can be contacted by mail at:
Sullivans Birmingham
5921 Greenwood parkway
Bessemer, AL 35023
276 734 5736

Coventry Spares Ltd.
John Healy
15 Abbey Lane,
Middleboro, MA 02346
1-800-451-5113

Hudson Cycle
Wakefield, MA
Don Hudson

Mitch Klempf
Klempf's British Parts
61589 210 Ave
Dodge Center, MN 55927
507 374 2222
www.klempfs.com

Sullivan, Bobby
can be contacted by mail at:
Sullivans
121 Franklin
Hanson, MA 02341

Shadley Brothers/Auto-Tec
1125 Bedford, Route 18
Whitman, MA 02382
781 447 2403

www.ingramcontent.com/pod-product-compliance
Lightning Source LLC
Chambersburg PA
CBHW062008150426
42812CB00013BA/2579